Liberating Jesus

Liberating Jesus

Christian Ethics for Privileged People

Kristopher Norris

t&tclark
LONDON • NEW YORK • OXFORD • NEW DELHI • SYDNEY

T&T CLARK

Bloomsbury Publishing Inc, 1359 Broadway, New York, NY 10018, USA
Bloomsbury Publishing Plc, 50 Bedford Square, London, WC1B 3DP, UK
Bloomsbury Publishing Ireland, 29 Earlsfort Terrace, Dublin 2, D02 AY28, Ireland

BLOOMSBURY, T&T CLARK and the T&T Clark logo are trademarks of
Bloomsbury Publishing Plc

First published in the United States of America 2026

Copyright © Bloomsbury Publishing Inc, 2018

For legal purposes the Acknowledgments on p. vii constitute an extension of this copyright page.

Cover design: Diana Nuhn
Cover image: painting "The One with the Crumby Dog"
(Urban Version) by Revd. Ally Barrett

All rights reserved. No part of this publication may be: i) reproduced or transmitted in any form, electronic or mechanical, including photocopying, recording or by means of any information storage or retrieval system without prior permission in writing from the publishers; or ii) used or reproduced in any way for the training, development or operation of artificial intelligence (AI) technologies, including generative AI technologies. The rights holders expressly reserve this publication from the text and data mining exception as per Article 4(3) of the Digital Single Market Directive (EU) 2019/790.

Bloomsbury Publishing Inc does not have any control over, or responsibility for, any third-party websites referred to or in this book. All internet addresses given in this book were correct at the time of going to press. The author and publisher regret any inconvenience caused if addresses have changed or sites have ceased to exist, but can accept no responsibility for any such changes.

Library of Congress Cataloging-in-Publication Data

ISBN: HB: 979-8-8818-0565-4
PB: 979-8-8818-0566-1
ePDF: 979-8-8818-6779-9
eBook: 979-8-8818-0567-8

Typeset by Deanta Global Publishing Services, Chennai, India
Printed and bound in the United States of America

For product safety related questions contact productsafety@bloomsbury.com.

To find out more about our authors and books visit www.bloomsbury.com and sign up for our newsletters.

For Alfredo
*This world needs your resilience, hope,
and happiness more than ever.*

CONTENTS

Prologue: The Beginnings, Ends, and Limits of Christian Ethics 1

Part I What Is Christian Ethics and How to Do It 13

1 Witness and Context 15

2 Models and Sources 35

3 Worship and Justice 55

Part II Christian Ethics in the World 75

4 Politics 77

5 War 97

6 Poverty 115

7 Patriarchy 131

8 White Supremacy 149

9 Climate Change 167

Epilogue: Ordinary Ethics 185

Bibliography 191
Index of Biblical References 195
Index 197
About the Author 200

Prologue

The Beginnings, Ends, and Limits of Christian Ethics

Woe to those who are at ease in Zion.

(AMOS 6:21)[1]

While working on this book, I received an invitation to speak to a local congregation on an ethics topic of my choice. I decided this would be a good opportunity to workshop Chapter 9 on environmental justice. This was one of the most progressive congregations in town (though I won't name the denomination here); mostly older and white, but leading the way on a lot of faith-based activism. When I arrived, I walked beneath a "Black Lives Matter" banner hanging above the narthex entry and passed by a poster announcing an upcoming community organizing training.

I began the presentation to a large Sunday School crowd. They laughed at my Kirk Cameron joke (you'll just have to wait for it!) and nodded in agreement with my analysis, until . . . I turned to ecofeminism and ecowomanism as constructive proposals for addressing climate change. White man after white man stood up to claim that race and gender had no role in addressing ecology, and that employing such theories only served to divide. Was I at the local Evangelical Bible Church? In fact, I received more pushback to my "racialized presentation" at this beacon of progressivism than when I had spoken on similar ethical topics at conservative churches. The idea that environmental injustice could be related to gender and racial injustice was too radical and political, and the turn to women and especially women of color for solutions seemed to be a step too far. No one was explicitly racist or sexist; they retreated into colorblindness and solutions rooted in capitalism. Yet, this experience with a group of progressive, mostly privileged people of faith only elevated my concern to write a book specifically for them—and for me. There is a long trajectory of Christianity inflicting harm upon the Earth and its most vulnerable people. Ignoring those oppressions in the present, and the ways they intersect and compound, risks repeating those same failures in the future. History echoes, if it is not examined and understood.

* * *

In 1554, three ships bearing the names of *Trinity*, *John the Evangelist*, and *Bartholomew* set sail for the coast of Guinea from an English port. These voyages, undertaken by Christian entrepreneurs on ships bearing theological titles hoping to mine the abundant resources of this "dark" continent, returned with five Africans, the first Black slaves to set foot in England.

As Joseph Washington comments, "Extracted from Africa and transported to England on waves of symbolism, these first black slaves were far from repulsive to Englishmen of Puritan pride and piety."[2] In just over half a century, the next generation of English colonialists would bring the first African slaves to the shores of the American colonies, sold to residents of Jamestown in 1619. By the turn of the nineteenth century, ships had brought three times as many enslaved Africans to the British colonies as white Europeans.[3] The Atlantic became a "conveyer belt to early death in the fields of an immense swath of plantations that stretched from Baltimore to Rio de Janeiro and beyond."[4] Before it was all over, between 10 and 15 million Africans would be ripped from their land and culture and imported to the New World, not counting those who perished in the Atlantic or in slave castles on African shores.

And many did die in these castles, the last stop and holding place of millions of Africans before they were prodded onto ships bound for the Americas. Many were forcibly baptized, stripped of their communal and familial identities, and bound sacramentally to their new white, Christian masters.[5] Christianity was not a means of abundant life for them; they were "buried in death by baptism" quite literally, as my Baptist baptismal liturgy proclaims, by a faith not their own. In one of these white-walled castles in Cape Coast,

Ghana, a slave dungeon sat directly beneath the chapel in which the European Christians held their worship services and praised God for their fortunes. At another castle in Elmina, "the slave auction block was literally beneath the chapel used for worship."[6] Reflecting on a visit to these spectacles, theologian and pastor Brad Braxton says the church was literally "propped up by the backs and bones of enslaved Africans." This is not only true regarding Christian slave traders in Africa but in America as well. The enslaved were not only responsible for building political institutions like the White House and Capitol but Christian institutions like Georgetown and Yale Universities. In fact, by 1767, the Catholic Jesuit order owned the greatest number of Africans of any institution in the Western Hemisphere.[7]

Like the dark waters of the Atlantic, the white church's baptismal waters are polluted with the blood of enslaved Africans and many others the church has oppressed over the centuries through Crusade, Inquisition, witch trials, anti-Semitism, Nazism, apartheid, and Jim Crow. But what has led Christians to such depths of depravity? As the names of the slave ships sailing on that "wave of symbolism" suggest, these forces of domination are rooted in Christian theology and promoted by Christian churches that have too often found themselves at the center of power and oppression.

But this seems a far cry from the original message of the Gospel, proclaimed well over a millennium earlier by the itinerant preacher who quickly became suspect to the powerful and good news to the oppressed. When Jesus returned to his hometown of Nazareth to officially begin his ministry, he first went to the synagogue. He stood up to read a mixture of selections from Isaiah: "The Spirit of the Lord is upon me, because he has anointed me to bring good news to the poor. He has sent me to proclaim release to the captives and recovery of sight to the blind, to let the oppressed go free, to proclaim the year of the Lord's favor" (Lk. 4:18-21). And then he told the crowd that this prophetic claim was fulfilled that day, in him.

Jesus' ministry begins not with a call to spiritual purity, a claim about getting to heaven, or even a command to love God, but with a message of liberation. In proclaiming the Year of the Lord's favor, Jesus is announcing the Jubilee year—the cycle established in Leviticus when the Israelites were to forgive all their debts and release their captives: a great reordering of society, one of redemption and liberation, that Jesus is now re-inaugurating (Lev. 25:8-22). And in doing this, Jesus is launching a great moral movement, a new way of life, a new social order, and even a new ethical reality by recalling the radical (if not aspirational) history of Israel. Jesus announces that God is restoring God's rule over Israel, now under the grip of the Roman Empire, and, through Israel, all of the Earth. The next three years of Jesus' ministry would begin to show just what this newly inaugurated order, this new ethical reality, would look like: dinners with outcasts, invitations to tax collectors, hope for the infirm and in-debt, lessons from outsiders, the high brought low and the lowly exalted, examples of sacrifice, compassion, and vulnerability. The type of actions that get deemed a threat by those in power.

"It cannot be denied that too often the weight of the Christian movement has been on the side of the strong and the powerful and against the weak and oppressed," lamented Howard Thurman, "this, despite the gospel."[8] So, what happened? The intervening two millennia since Jesus' life and ministry call into question the legacy of Christianity and the failure of Christian ethics to produce people who follow in the way of Jesus. As most data suggest a great contemporary exodus from the church and general dissatisfaction with organized Christianity, there exists an urgent question of whether 2,000 years of Christianity have done more harm than good upon the Earth and its people. I have written elsewhere of the ways Christianity produced colonialism, white supremacy, and the Atlantic Slave Trade and continues to perpetuate racism today.[9] One recent study provides evidence that going to church actually makes people more racist.[10] Large segments of Christianity continue to endorse discrimination against women, the LGBTQ community, and other marginalized groups; underwrite a capitalist system that destroys the planet and renders portions uninhabitable; and manufacture a complex, individualized approach to poverty that promotes charity work but resists structural engagement. Christianity has done much harm in the name of Jesus. In fact, for at least the past thousand years, the mission of Jesus has been captive to a colonial ethic of exploitation and oppression that has contorted and distorted much of Christian theology and the practice of ministry. Christians, especially those of us with social and political privilege, have gotten too comfortable in Zion, if not used it to prop up ourselves through the exploitation and oppression of others. This dark reality leads theologian and priest Kelly Brown Douglas to begin her book, *What's Faith Got to Do with It?* with the question: if Christianity has been used for centuries to oppress people, "Was there not something wrong with Christianity itself?"[11]

Liberating Jesus seeks to address this ambiguous reality. This book issues a call to liberate Jesus from this oppressive ethic of domination. In other words, *Liberating Jesus* enjoins Christians with privilege and power to promote a liberative Christian ethic that serves as a corrective to the harms Christianity has manifested and conventional Christian ethics has neglected or even supported. The purpose of this book is to provide an accessible, unique framework for understanding a Christian ethic of liberation that engages privileged people in the work of liberating others, and in so doing, liberating ourselves. This is not a conventional textbook in that it is not meant to be objective or neutral. While it will touch on a variety of theories or approaches, it will not provide a comprehensive overview. As you will come to see, I have particular commitments that animate and drive the framework presented in this book. It serves as a guide for one way of *doing* Christian ethics—that is deliberating about how to think about the moral life, what issues matter, how much agency we have, what limits ought to be set, what practices and habits are shaping us (and what practices and habits ought to shape us), and how to respond to realities, both quotidian and crisis.

This book also proposes Christian ethics not as some abstract academic exercise but as a field of inquiry that inevitably affects you and your ministry every day in some way or another. Whether we frame ethical concerns in terms of "What would Jesus do?," "What does justice require?," or "What type of community do we need to be?," ministry is a profoundly ethical vocation, and so I believe we need to become more familiar with the deep resources— and the limits—of our Christian tradition to help guide us as we seek to become better disciples, ministers, and followers of Christ.

* * *

Walter Brueggemann wrote a wonderful little prayer book titled, *Prayers for a Privileged People*, from which this book takes its inspiration—and its subtitle. That volume contains prayers of lament and hope, including one asking that "we find our privilege eroded by your purpose ... our entitlement unsettled by your other children." Brueggemann explains his hope for the prayers in that volume: "As we acknowledge our privilege, name our anxieties, and recognize our brothers and sisters, we are surprised by a call from God. Rather than autonomous agents of self-regard in the world, we are gifted by, belong with, and answer to another. This other, the Holy One, sends our life off in new directions . . . out beyond our privilege. Thus, such prayer summons us to get our minds off ourselves, to ponder the God who gives us life, and who dispatches us for the sake of the lives of others."[12]

In that same spirit, I write this book on an ethic for privileged Christians, hoping to conjure a similar "summons" to move privileged people beyond. I'll address who that refers to over the next three chapters, as a privileged Christian myself. I am a white, upper-middle-class, highly educated man who lives on a peaceful cul-de-sac in a nice city surrounded by loving family and friends. I have never experienced an urgent financial crisis or safety issues and have no idea what the trauma of those types of experiences is like. I have a fairly strong anti-authority streak that has gotten me into trouble on many occasions (I once wore duct-tape shoes to my office job in protest over a dress code policy and took my church youth group to a drag bingo show, but those are stories for another book). But such actions have never cost me materially, and were certainly emboldened by my social location and sense of entitlement. I have served as a pastor, youth minister, denominational staff, seminary professor, and nonprofit worker. I have journeyed from conservative, Evangelical Southern Baptist to a member of a very progressive (though mostly white) faith community committed to the work of anti-racism in response to the Gospel. This book is confessional, shaped by years of mistakes and missteps: moving too slowly to embrace a commitment to justice, ignoring my blind spots to racism and sexism, struggling to come to grips with the depth of the systemic injustices around us and Christianity's role in creating and sustaining them. As the white Episcopalian theologian and activist William Stringfellow concluded after observing white churches "as having no viable word to say in the present crisis or, beyond that, of not having the courage or integrity to act"—*My people is the en*emy.[13] I do not write this as a scholar who has escaped my own privilege, nor as one who writes from the margins myself. I write as a privileged person primarily for other privileged Christians and hopefully turn attention to those who are writing from the margins as I do so. This book is my way of exploring sources and frameworks that might lead enemies like myself to liberate ourselves from our privilege on the way to liberating those that privileged Christians have pushed to the margins, ignored, and harmed.

The path I chart in this book is, in a sense, to reconcile two seemingly divergent and influential theological frameworks. I grew up Baptist and in seminary gravitated to the communal, pacifist perspective of Anabaptism. This led me quite easily to embrace the traditionalist and virtue ethics approach of postliberal theology. Postliberalism was an attempt to correct for what some mid-twentieth-century theologians saw as accommodation to the culture of liberalism and its thin Christology and sense of community within major theological movements like the Social Gospel and Christian Realism. While highlighting a strong view of the church as a community maintaining distinctive practices that inform the way it interprets and responds to the world, postliberalism was a retrieval of what came before liberalism, namely tradition, orthodoxy, community, and character. While much of this perspective still informs my work, I have come to resist the tendency to let these commitments lead to a strong division between the "church" and the "world," with an often-closed mission to protect the church from the world by maintaining distinctive practices and commitments. I'm haunted by my assent to a major postliberal thinker's maxim: "Let the church be the church and the world be the world."

In graduate school and during my first years of teaching, various events signaled holes in this approach: police shootings of unarmed Black men, growing cultural disdain for immigrants and refugees, skyrocketing wealth inequality, and reckless neglect of the Earth and its future generations. One event, the white supremacist rally while I was living in Charlottesville, Virginia in 2017, was a major turning point as I witnessed the absence and silence of most local churches in condemnation of racism and support of the counter-protesters and activists—churches I had grown to value and love. The problems of injustice were intertwined, systemic, and deeper than I had imagined, and a postliberal theology and ethics that seemed so focused inward was insufficient to address them. Postliberalism was, after all, written and produced primarily by privileged white male scholars.

While writing my dissertation, I had also developed a relationship with James Cone, professor at Union Theological Seminary in NY and father of Black Liberation Theology. I gradually began to see the way liberation theology recognized the intersectional and systemic nature of injustice in ways to which I had been blind. Liberation theology responded to the same mid-century shortcomings in conventional theology, especially as the civil rights, women's, and antiwar movements were growing. It pushed Christian theology toward a more activist posture, underscoring the overcoming of oppression for the poor and marginalized as the core mission of Christianity by listening to and highlighting the marginalized voices within theology—Black, Latin American, queer, feminist, and womanist (or Black women scholars responding to the dual and intersecting oppressions of patriarchy and racism). These theologians sought to retrieve the embodied and prophetic characteristics of the Gospel as the good news of liberation to the poor and oppressed. The church exists only insofar as it works actively to secure this liberation.

At first glance, these seem to be two divergent paradigms of theological formation that have also influenced polarized developments within the church as well. The church then is left with the seemingly exclusive pastoral options of focusing on tradition or injustice, minds or bodies, the "not-yet" or "already" of the coming salvation of God. But this does not have to be so. *Liberating Jesus* identifies the commonalities between these threads, notably the importance of community, character, and justice—while acknowledging their distinctions—and directs them toward the target audience: Christians who embody and enjoy various levels of social, economic, and political privilege. In doing so, it calls on us to confront the oppressive legacy of Christian ethics and begin to understand ethics as formation into a life of service and advocacy, following the witness of Jesus, for the liberation of the marginalized. The *communitarian virtue ethic of liberation* proposed in this book draws on resources from both perspectives and, with the help of the "both-and" approach of womanist ethics, demonstrates that they are not only compatible sources but provide privileged Christians with a path toward ethical thinking and action that works for the liberation of the oppressed and liberates ourselves from our own blindness and biases.

Part I of the book lays the groundwork for this ethical approach. The book begins with an argument for the contextuality of ethics, not as an abstract set of principles to be applied universally, but as a formation that arises out of the lived experience and context of a particular community's moral reasoning. The first chapter defines ethics as formation into a life of witness and justice, recognizing the centrality of context. Chapter 2 analyzes sources, here redefined as "witnesses" to the Christian Gospel, and conventional approaches to ethics, revealing that this book foregrounds a character/virtue model. The final step of the methodology section is to link worship and justice. A virtue approach to ethics recognizes the connection between the practices of faith—liturgy, as the work of the people—and the work of doing justice in the world. Part II takes this communitarian liberation virtue ethic, with particular attention given to the contextuality of moral concerns and intersectionality of approaches, and engages with six pressing contemporary concerns: political engagement, war and peace, racial justice, economic justice, gender and patriarchy, and climate change. Each chapter models the way someone formed within this communitarian virtue ethic of liberation might address and respond to these issues.

In this book, you will find resources in surprising places. For example, virtue ethics from womanist scholars, the theology of Stanley Hauerwas helping to confront patriarchy, and politics in the work of a children's ministry. Hopefully, you will find yourself challenged, encouraged, and pushed to new perspectives. In the midst of the Holocaust, Jewish writer Elie Wiesel wondered if God was dead; the German pastor and theologian Dietrich Bonhoeffer wondered the same about the church. Witnessing its failure to confront the Nazi agenda, he questioned if all that should be left of this fragile institution was "prayer" and "righteous action."[14] In some ways, the microcosm of the Holocaust is a witness to the larger, centuries-long failure of Christianity to live up to the message and witness of Jesus. Christianity needs liberating, and this can come only from voices both inside and outside the tradition, from a wide witness of perspectives and experiences. It is with this witness of perspectives and experiences that we begin in Chapter 1.

Notes

1 New American Standard Bible version (all scripture references will be from the NRSV unless otherwise noted).
2 Joseph R. Washington, *Anti-Blackness in English Religion, 1500–1800* (Lewiston, NY: Edwin Mellen Press, 1984), 107.

3 Rolando Mellafe, *La esclavitud en Hispanoamerica* (Buenos Aires: EUDEBA, 1964), 59–60; cited in Rivera, 182; Adam Hochschild, *Bury the Chains: Prophets and Rebels in the Fight to Free an Empire's Slaves* (Boston: Mariner Books, 2006), 3.

4 Hochschild, *Bury the Chains*, 3.

5 Orlando Patterson, *Slavery and Social Death: A Comparative Study*, 1st ed. (Cambridge, MA: Harvard University Press, 1985), 8–9; Saidiya Hartman, *Lose Your Mother: A Journey Along the Atlantic Slave Route* (New York: Farrar, Straus & Giroux, 2008).

6 Brad R. Braxton, "Lifting the Veil: The *Shoah* and the *Maafa* in Conversation," *Perspectives in Religious Studies* 38, no. 2 (2011): 188. Information on Elmina from Hartman, 58. She notes that by 1540, between ten and twenty thousand slaves had been confined within the walls of the fort (62).

7 Frederick P. Bowser, "Africans in Spanish American Colonial Society," in *The Cambridge History of Latin America*, vol. 11, ed. Leslie Bethell (Cambridge, UK: Cambridge University Press, 1986), 371.

8 Howard Thurman, *Jesus and the Disinherited* (Boston: Beacon Press, 1996), 31.

9 See "To See Responsibility from Below: Bonhoeffer, Niebuhr, and Race," *Theology Today* 80, no. 2 (2023): 144–61; *Witnessing Whiteness: Confronting White Supremacy in the American Church* (Oxford: Oxford University Press, 2020); "Witnessing Whiteness in the Ethics of Hauerwas," *Journal of Religious Ethics* 47, no. 1 (2019): 117–42.

10 Robert P. Jones, *White Too Long: The Legacy of White Supremacy in American Christianity* (New York: Simon & Schuster, 2020). Jones developed a "Racism Index" derived from the responses to questions about systemic racism: opinions on Confederate monuments, the racial wealth gap, inequality in the criminal justice system, and police killings, for example. White Evangelicals scored the highest on this Racism Index, despite a self-perception of warmth toward African Americans. White mainline and Catholic Christians fared no better than Evangelicals—scoring only slightly lower on the Racism Index. Jones summarizes it: on a scale of 0–1, white Evangelicals scored 0.78, white Catholics 0.72, and white mainline Protestants 0.69, compared to white religiously unaffiliated Americans at 0.42. This means that white Christians as a whole register as more racist than white non-religious Americans, "and the differences between white Christian subgroups (white Evangelical Protestants, white mainline Protestants, and white Catholics) are largely differences of degree rather than kind," 169–171.

11 Kelly Brown Douglas, *What's Faith Got to Do with It? Black Bodies/ Christian Souls* (Maryknoll, NY: Orbis Books, 2005), xiii.

12 Walter Brueggemann, *Prayers for a Privileged People* (Nashville: Abingdon Press, 2008), 45, xiv–xv.

13 William Stringfellow, *My People is the Enemy: An Autobiographical Polemic* (Eugene: Wipf and Stock, 2005), 138.

14 Dietrich Bonhoeffer, *Letters and Papers from Prison, Dietrich Bonhoeffer Works (English)*, vol. 8, ed. John W. de Gruchy, trans. Reinhard Krauss, Nancy Lukens, Lisa E. Dahill, and Isabel Best (Minneapolis, MN: Fortress Press, 2010), 389.

PART I

What Is Christian Ethics and How to Do It

1

Witness and Context

Introduction: A Superior Discipline

One morning a visitor arrived at Finkenwalde, the illegal seminary that Dietrich Bonhoeffer had founded near the Baltic coast in the summer of 1935. Bonhoeffer was a Lutheran pastor and theologian who had opposed the Nazi takeover of German churches. He had helped nurture the fledgling Confessing Church movement that attempted to resist Nazi theology and eventually would join a conspiracy to kill Adolf Hitler, before ultimately being executed in a concentration camp. Bonhoeffer's permission to teach in official universities had already been revoked by the Nazi government, but he felt compelled to continue training Confessing Church pastors for the impending struggle against the Nazis.

This visitor, an old friend of Bonhoeffer, toured the seminary, observing the community members cleaning, studying, praying, singing—the daily rhythms and discipline that constituted their communal and educational life together: a regimen that initially drew the charge of "legalism" from disgruntled seminarians![1] His friend remarked that there was so much focus on discipline; where was room for pleasure, for cinema, for play? The next morning, Bonhoeffer took this visitor rowing on the sound just a few miles from the seminary. They stopped near some dunes and climbed them until they could see below a field with runways of German fighter jets and Nazi military formations performing their morning exercises. Bonhoeffer told him that there was an entire generation of Germans in training, whose disciplines were formed "for a kingdom . . . of hardship and cruelty." For Christians to have a chance to resist this, he told his friend, it would require another form of politics shaped by a "superior discipline."[2]

Bonhoeffer called his short-lived experiment in theological education at Finkenwalde a "proving ground." In fact, his book, *Life Together*, which outlines the practices of Finkenwalde, begins with a sort of mission statement for the seminary: Christians belong "not in the seclusion of cloistered life, but in the midst of enemies."[3] As Bonhoeffer scholar Geffrey Kelly notes, "[Bonhoeffer] intended their life together to be a unique, more effective way of preparing these young ministers to enter that struggle [against Nazism] . . . and in the process to revitalize their church."[4]

It is interesting that Bonhoeffer invokes political, even military language to describe the Christian life. Of course, such a description cannot be removed from its socio-political context during the Church Struggle in the early years of the Third Reich, where signs of political oppression were emerging and the nationalist "German Christian" churches were actively supporting the Nazi regime. Yet, the fact that these were extraordinary times with their own particular forms of crisis and conflict does not mean that we do not live in our own extraordinary times, with our own particular (and perhaps congruent) forms of crisis and conflict.

Some of this crisis and conflict is seen and experienced on the political level: we are reminded daily, with every news report, of the growing political divisions and endless crises in government; we witness government-sanctioned racial oppression at the border and in the streets and even courtrooms; and we understand the divergent ways various theological and ecclesial institutions have chosen to respond to these issues. In fact, one way to make sense of the radically disparate Christian responses to public crisis, and of the church's political engagement altogether, is to consider the ways Christian leaders are and have been trained in moral reflection—in fact, to understand ethics as a training or a formation (and sometimes a malformation) into a way of life.

Witness: Christianity as a Way of Life

This book on Christian ethics begins in an unusual place—at the beginning. Rather than start the first chapter with modern methodologies or sources for thinking morally, I'm beginning with the concept of witness, which I understand to be the original framework with which the disciples and early church considered the Christian life. At the origins of Christianity, the early Christians understood their faith not primarily as a set of beliefs, but as a way of life. I believe *witness* is a helpful way to think about ethics still today because it directly connects ethics to other disciplines in theological education and practice—theology, church history, ministry, and mission. Ethics does not stand alone as an independent subject, separate from these other elements, but interacts with all of these others to shape the Christian life of discipleship and the vocation of ministry. There are three distinctive meanings of *witness* that are important to understand as we move along.

The idea of witness in some conservative and Evangelical circles has taken on the narrow definition of *proselytizing*. It is sharing a testimony of one's salvation or sharing the faith in a way that hopes to convert the other person—getting them saved! I remember growing up in a conservative Evangelical congregation in which I participated in weekly evangelism nights. A group of us would cold call a recent visitor to the church or a friend of a church member who "needed saving," and this poor, unsuspecting soul would be forced to sit and listen to one of us provide personal testimony of how our life had been changed and pearly gates were secured by accepting Jesus into our heart. We gave "witness" to the Gospel through our words--and by wearing our "Jesus Saves" T-shirts so others would see and come to know the glory of Jesus.

Second, and important for this study, the concept of witness has also become especially prominent in postliberal theology—one of my primary formative frameworks and one that has influenced much of contemporary Christian theology even if it is not directly named. Here it is often expressed in narrow, triumphalist rhetoric: witnessing to the Gospel before a world that has rejected it. In this tradition, witness is not so much about proselytizing as it is about the distinctive moral witness of the church in contrast to a world that lives by other commitments—demonstrating to a sinful world what it means to live a godly life. This is witness as providing a *moral example*. In this framework, a focus on the distinctive and unique witness of the church works to establish a strong boundary between church and world—an understanding of the church's radical separation from the world.

Yet, there is a third understanding of witness: not witnessing to others through word or lifestyle, but witnessing others. This is bearing witness of what others have to teach us—witnessing as in *seeing, listening to,* and *learning from.* This understanding of witness recognizes the limits of what we know, that we see this world and our place in it through a mirror dimly (1 Cor. 13:12), and need others—those outside of our community (especially as privileged people)—to open up our perspective beyond our lenses.

I believe that witness may be a broadly useful ethical concept, and one that will guide the examination of Christian ethics in this book. Each of these meanings of witness plays an important role in Christian faith today. In building a communitarian virtue ethics of liberation, I am going to focus on the second two meanings in this book, witness as a) moral example and b) as seeing and learning from. In fact, I will integrate them as much as I can in order to break down the sharp distinction in postliberalism between the church and the world. I think any task of Christian moral formation requires a balance between concern over the internal sources of one's own moral formation and listening to and responding to those outside of that community who provide the most accurate and instructive reflection to one's dimly lit lens. So, to begin grappling with this idea and way of thinking about ethics as witness, I want to start at the beginning of Christianity to show how this idea of witness unites theology, ethics, and ministry. We see this focus on witness in some of the earliest writings—especially in one that I think is often, and unfortunately, overlooked.

The *Didache*

The *Didache* was collected and written down somewhere between 50–80 CE, around the same time or even preceding the dates some of the New Testament Gospels were written. It outlines the liturgical instructions and ethical practices of the early church and what they understood to be the most significant factors for conversion. It begins, "There are two ways: one of life and one of death! And there is a great difference between the two ways." The *Didache* then focuses on practices, on ethics, on converting to a particular and peculiar way of life rather than accepting certain beliefs in order to be part of the Christian community, as many have come to read parts of the New Testament as prescriptive. It talks of Christianity as a way of "training" that involves behaviors like turning the other cheek, praying for enemies, going the extra mile, not coveting or gambling, and joining the Christian community through practices of baptism, prayer, and Eucharist.

You might be wondering, why begin with such an obscure text? This often overlooked work shows us that Christianity, from the beginning, was not primarily a matter of intellectual agreement with a set of beliefs or propositions about God or Jesus. It took centuries and many, many councils for the Church to decide definitively on the details of orthodox beliefs about who Jesus was and how he related to God. By the time it determined these doctrines, there were already large numbers of Christians who had joined the church not simply because they believed its claims about Jesus and its promises of eternal life, but also *and especially* because they were attracted to the way of life they saw Christians practicing. In this view, the life of the church and the work of Christian ethics began primarily as a matter of public *witness*.

Becoming Christian was a decision to follow Jesus, meaning: to behave in ways that imitated his example, to respond to the world around them in ways that modeled his responses, to engage in practices and a lifestyle that would train them to conform to his character. For early Christians, that is what believing in Jesus meant: the conviction that following Jesus' example and teaching was the good and right way to live and would result in lasting peace and happiness—even including a life after death—and that, somehow, Jesus enabled his followers to live such a life. This belief was spread at least as much by the example of Christians living what appeared to be good, happy, and peaceful lives—perhaps at times also sacrificial if the circumstances called for such a bold example—as by the preaching of the Gospel message.

Conversions to Christianity were thus, to a large extent, *moral conversions*; the beliefs were accepted because they appeared to lead to a kind of life that many people wanted for themselves. The way of life Christians practiced was considered their primary witness to the veracity of their beliefs. Christianity began as a moral movement, and its theological claims and doctrines developed in tandem with interpretations of how Jesus wanted his followers to live.

Interpreting Jesus

So far, this might sound like that triumphalist postliberal moral vision of witness I previously criticized. And that's why understanding ethics as witness inevitably leads to the question of how to interpret Jesus in order to know what it means and looks like to follow him. What Jesus said and did during his years of ministry on Earth, recorded in the Gospels and in some letters of the early apostles, is unquestionably the root of Christian ethics. They are relayed to us largely through the genre of story, and these stories are unquestionably up for interpretation. Christian ethics deals with what it means to become part of these ongoing stories, manifest in a particular community that understands them in light of their own context. The history of Christian ethics is, in many ways, a history of how Jesus' sayings and actions have been interpreted over time—a study, that is, of the ongoing differences and disagreements about how they are to be understood. For the earliest churches, with Jesus no longer bodily present, the dominant question was: What does Jesus' life and message mean for the particular, day-to-day moral behavior of Jesus' followers?

This question of interpretation does not go away, but has to be handled by every generation of Christians. And it means, most directly, that we must proceed with grace and humility. Christian ethics cannot be understood over against the world, but as a faith seeking understanding within a messy and complex world. I don't have all the answers, but my witness must be open to yours, and together we learn. It is important to understand who the historical Jesus was, as the theologian James Cone tells us, but also to understand who Jesus Christ is for us today, in our different contexts. We understand that our interpretation is limited, and we might have things to learn from others.

The Gospels of Matthew and Mark provide us with a unique story in the life of Jesus—not one of him liberating others but a story of liberating Jesus, perhaps from his own parochial bias? As he has ventured into Gentile territory, a Canaanite woman approaches asking him to heal her daughter (Mt. 15:21-28 and Mk 7:24-30). Actually, the woman is shouting, "Have mercy on me, Lord, Son of David; my daughter is tormented by a demon." Jesus at first ignores her inappropriate outburst and then responds, "I was sent only to the lost sheep of the house of Israel." Gaining her composure, she kneels next to Jesus and again begs him for help. This time he offers one of the most perplexing lines in the Gospels: "It is not fair to take the children's food and throw it to the dogs." (Earlier in Matthew's Gospel, Jesus had forbidden his followers from giving what is holy to dogs—a deeply offensive image for outsiders in the ancient world.) Undeterred by his rather hostile insult, the woman replies, "Yes, Lord, yet even the dogs eat the crumbs that fall from their masters' table." At this, Jesus praises her faith and heals her daughter. In an almost improvisationally-motivated step, the Canaanite woman over-accepts Jesus' insult, concedes the point, and presses forward: "Yes, and?" Even in the face of a verbal wall of ethnic division, nevertheless, she persisted. While many preachers want to sanitize this story and claim that Jesus was joking, there is no evidence of that. The historical Jesus was one who learned from outsiders, and this woman's move to defend the rights of her people to the liberation that Jesus offers impresses the Teacher and wins the day. Jesus bears her witness. He listens and learns from her witness, and is changed by the encounter. And just as Jesus listened to marginalized others and allowed their witness to shape his own, we should allow ourselves—and our interpretations of the Gospel—to be formed by other voices.

The question of interpretation and context inevitably leads to the question of the public nature of Christian faith and its ethics. How ought we relate to the world around us and within us? There were two kinds of issues at stake for the early Christians. One could be called the relation between "now and then"—the question of eschatology: What difference did anything done or achieved in this world make to the afterlife? The other was the relation between "us and them"—the question of identity: How were Christians supposed to relate to non-Christians, and Christianity to non-Christian society? This quandary raised very specific questions about whether one could be both Christian and a soldier, or a merchant, or a civil servant (like a tax collector for the Empire). At a social level, Christians wondered whether they were called to work toward transforming society into a kind of Christian commonwealth or theocracy, or whether they should withdraw from pagan society as much as possible to maintain their own moral integrity. (I'll argue a few chapters later against both of these extremes!)

There is much more that can be written here, but from this brief account of the early church's approach to ethics, we see that

Christian ethics cannot be separated from Christian theology, and Christian ethics is far from monolithic. There is no easy demarcation between action and belief in Christianity. Christian ethics is tethered to the particularities of Christian belief, the Christian community, and Christian witness or way of life. It is the outworking of Christian belief within one's own situation, in witness to what we might learn from others. Theology and ethics go hand in hand, mutually influencing each other. Christian belief is faith seeking understanding of our particular way of life in the world within the context we find ourselves.

The Role of Context

Sometimes, however, a focus on the witness of the church neglects the role of context in theology. If we understand witness as proselytizing or as a universal and objective moral example against a sinful world, ethics is simply applying a set of objective values to a situation. But this does not take seriously enough the role of experience and the power of our own social conditioning. The particular daily reality in which I live not only animates the moral conclusions I come to but also the ethical questions that confront me and the tools of interpretation available to me. A universal and objective understanding of witness neglects the fact that the Gospels and epistles we use for our moral reasoning themselves offer stories and instructions from a variety of contexts, often presenting conflicting accounts and prescribing conflicting advice: for example, in one Gospel Jesus warns the Pharisees, "Whoever is not with me is against me" (Mt. 12:30) but then in another he tells his disciple John, "Whoever is not against us is for us" (Mk 9:40). Thus, it may seem counterintuitive to talk about the role of context in ethical reasoning before providing an overview of the various approaches or models of ethics, but I believe addressing this crucial topic first will help us properly and critically assess the most significant and traditional models of ethics and sources of authority in ethics.

Context inevitably matters for how we think about ethics: it matters for how we interpret Jesus and his teaching and example, how we understand the relation of the church to the world, and how we understand the ways our way of life is shaped by our faith. Ethics and theology may be inseparable, but so are ethics and social context.

For example, as a white, upper-middle-class man with a graduate education, my daily reality of privilege influences the sphere of my concerns, the problems I see around me, the questions I ask about those problems, and the way I understand them to impact myself and others. It limits my knowledge, narrows my purview, and shapes my analysis. For instance, in graduate school, I set out to write a dissertation on the political engagement of the church in America. I was comparing and contrasting two scholars on this issue, one of whom was James Cone, who has informed much of the content of this book as well. Cone is considered the Father of Black Liberation Theology; his work and theology of the church are permeated by the experience of racism. Yet, in my doctoral engagement with his ecclesiology, that is, his study of the nature and work of the church, I did not address race or racism. The entire 300,000-word thesis did not even contain the word *race*. My own context limited and even blinded me. I knew churches were generally segregated, but from my position of white privilege, I never had to consider the impact that racism, white supremacy, and the history of slavery and Jim Crow had on the political engagement of congregations. I needed experiences and exposure—Ferguson, MO, Charlottesville, VA, reading more womanist theologians and scholars of color—to show me my blind spots. I still continue to write out of that position, with all of its limitations, but hope to point to the witness of others who can better light our way.

This is why I argue that context, including the memory of our own suffering and oppression, as well as our sins and oppression of others, are key to Christian witness. Proper witness is not only a positive demonstration of what it means to live in Christian community, but also, for many of us, a confessional one that witnesses to the importance of repentance.

The Contextual Nature of Ethics

One of the best examples of the importance of context in ethical thinking comes from the late womanist ethicist Katie Cannon. Her key insight is that one "must always take into account the circumstances, the paradoxes and the dilemmas" that shape one's situation and context when considering moral agency. "The real-lived texture of Black life requires moral agency that may run contrary to the ethical boundaries of mainline Protestantism," she argues. "Blacks may use action guides which have never been considered within the scope of traditional codes of faithful living." Their situation under oppression means that the marginalized must "create and cultivate values and virtues in their own terms" in order to be able to live, deliberate, and act "with moral integrity." For example, dominant ethics venerate a virtue of suffering as a desirable moral norm, calling its proponents toward voluntary suffering on behalf of the neighbor. In privileged Christian circles, "one is free to choose whether or not she/he wants to suffer and make sacrifices" as an act of cross-bearing. But, "for the masses of Black people, suffering is the normal state of affairs." Prescribing more voluntary suffering for a people who cannot choose otherwise is not a moral good. In this context, acts of resistance might be more virtuous.[5]

She demonstrates from the wisdom of enslaved Black women that ethics should not "appeal to the fixed rules or absolute principles of what is right or wrong or good or bad." Rather, communities must "embrace values related to the causal conditions of their cultural circumstances." She continues, "The cherished assumptions of dominant ethical systems predicated upon both the existence of freedom and a wide range of choices have proven to be false in the real-lived texture of Black life." Cannon recalls the ways enslaved women refused the docile moral precepts exhorted by slave preachers but "learned to consider their vices as virtues in their dealing with whites."[6] Cannon's method for womanist ethics is to begin with experience rather than theories or norms. For her, experiential themes generate ethical implications that can lead to "norms lived out in the realities of day-to-day experience."[7]

Affirming their God-granted dignity denied to them in their moral situation of oppression under slavery, these women developed an ethic focused on survival as their central virtue. Virtue involved deceiving the master in order to avoid punishment or looking for means of escape whenever possible. Actions deemed deviant by white society were virtuous in the ethical code developed within the concrete situation of the Black community, suggesting the particular and communal shape of ethics.

Her crucial point is that all ethics is contextual. What is moral, what is the ethically appropriate action, how ought we to think ethically about this or that, and how should we live given this set of realities? These questions can only be identified and discerned within the particular situation and social condition of the community in which one lives. What is virtuous action for someone in the situation of oppression may not be virtuous for someone else. From another context, the Nazi-era German theologian and ethicist Dietrich Bonhoeffer highlighted above—a theologian who has become even more popular in recent years as some have deemed these times of political and moral uncertainty a "Bonhoeffer moment"—also emphasized the contextual nature of ethics. For him, ethics entails a concrete response within the situation in which a moral agent finds oneself. Because an individual only exists in relationship to an Other, Bonhoeffer writes, a "person exists always and only in ethical responsibility."[8] He insists that humans do not live independently or "unmediated," but live "in responsibility vis-à-vis an 'other.'" The ethical person does not act upon a predetermined set of universal moral principles, but the moral action "grows out of the concrete situation" and recognizes the ethical demands and boundaries presented by the concrete other.[9]

In an essay he wrote from a Nazi prison after being arrested on suspicions of participating in a plot to assassinate Adolf Hitler, on "What It Means to Tell the Truth," Bonhoeffer goes so far as to claim that the context or situation in which a moral agent finds herself determines the moral choice. He gives the example of a student in a classroom misleading or providing what we would consider a lie about her family life to her teacher. He claims that would not in fact be a lie because—in technical theological terms—it is none of the teacher's damn business. Providing false information to a nosy teacher about the intimacies of family life would not be a lie, whereas doing so to one's parent would be a lie.[10] What is a lie in one context is a truth in another; the situation, and the concrete person one is engaging, determine the morality of a statement. Now, there are overarching frameworks governing Bonhoeffer's reason for this that we don't need to get into at this point, but the central concern is that for Christian ethicists as divergent as a white, bourgeois mid-century German theologian to a womanist ethicist writing fifty years later in the American South, an emphasis on the importance of context in Christian ethics is a central and foregrounding concern. And this pertains to *all* of Christian theology.

To some, this may sound like moral relativism—anything goes and there is no objective moral truth. But that goes too far.

What Cannon, Bonhoeffer, and others who advocated for this contextual approach understood is that each community asks these questions and seeks moral truth by drawing on the sources of Christian faith and witness—scripture, reason, experience, tradition; who Jesus was and who Jesus is for us today. This was true of the early church that produced the *Didache*, and it is true of every Christian community today.

When I was in seminary, it was popular to talk about "contextual theologies," and in many institutions of theological education, it still is. "Contextual theologies" included Black theology, liberation theology, queer theology, feminist, mujerista, and womanist theology. These theologies were driven by one's context and social location when, presumably, white, male American and European theologies were not. The trend in the academy of identifying Black, feminist, queer, or liberation theologies as "contextual theologies" reinforces the false notion that classic European (white) theology is universal, objective, and normative. This belief, however, has led to much harm. Womanist theologian Stacey Floyd-Thomas argues that the "universalizing" idea of virtue promoted by most white, male theologians only brings about "desired ends for members of the privileged class," but not the dispossessed.[11] It is often in the privileged group's best interest to ignore contextuality and promote an abstract and universal ethic that leaves context unquestioned. This has been the pattern of Christian ethics for most of history, which is why a Christian ethic for those of us who enjoy various forms of privilege—social, economic, political—must begin from the standpoint of context. But we can clearly see, and recent history makes this too apparent, that all theologies and ethics are "contextual." We each have a context, a social location, that conditions and may sometimes determine the ethical responses and outcomes at which we arrive.

James Cone on Context

And here enters James Cone again, a primary interlocutor for this book. Writing over a 50-year period from the civil rights era until his passing in 2019, he consistently identifies and argues for the contextual nature of all theology. Similar to many Latin American liberation theologians like Gustavo Gutiérrez, he argues that theology emerges from the socio-religious experience of a particular community. There is no objective theology; theological speech is always a product of its social environment, limited by history, place, and time, and the particularity of our existence. Context becomes a crucial part of understanding the church's witness when you begin to think about the way that a minister's, theologian's, or community's context—its social, ethnic, historical context—shapes the beliefs and practices of the community, including its theology and ethics. All of us are story-shaped people. The multiple stories in which one lives shape one's identity and sense of values, helping us interpret how we perceive the world and receive the ideas and practices it gives us.

In other words, theology and ethics do not come to us unaffected by our social condition. Cone argues that we should not understand revelation to be a deposit of pure, fixed doctrines because there is no truth outside of the concrete historical events in which people are engaged as agents. Divine revelation is never pure or unmediated but is always filtered through our social conditioning and experience. In this sense, theology is critical reflection upon a people's prior affirmations and political commitments. In other words, theology is not primary but second order reflection on prior cultural and political positions. In many ways, it reveals more about the theologian and her context than it does about God.

Cone appeals to the intellectual heritage of philosophers like Ludwig Feuerbach and Karl Marx to argue for the contextuality of intellectual thought. As Marxist philosopher Howard Selsam puts it, "the ethics of any age is an outgrowth of, and is relevant to, the actual conditions of life of that age, and therefore the examination of these must precede any attempt to judge morally or to set significant norms."[12] Building on this approach, Cone writes, "Theology is subjective speech about God, a speech that tells us far more about the hopes and dreams of certain God-talkers than about the Maker and Creator of heaven and earth."[13] Ideas do not have independent existence but are a social product of theologians' reflections about divine things and are always intertwined with manifestations of actual life. He appeals to liberation theologian Gustavo Gutiérrez's claim that, "Theology is done by persons who, whether they know it or not, are caught up in particular social processes. Consequently, all theology is in part a reflection of this or that concrete process. Theology is not something disembodied or atemporal."[14]

Cone does not deny objectivity or objective truth per se; only that objectivity remains elusive to humans who are inevitably finite and incapable of transcending our context. But this also means that theological language is always "interested"—by which he means it is shaped by the perspective and goals of the one doing the theological speaking. Womanist theologian Emilie Townes argues effectively that "the act of knowing is always contextual." Knowledge, including theological knowledge, can never be objective or disinterested, but is "fraught with our best and worst impulses," and therefore, can become dangerous when that contextuality is ignored or unexamined.[15]

This leads Cone to emphasize the political nature of theology, that one's theology reflects one's political status and interests.[16] Again, as Townes asserts, our political judgments inevitably contain implicit theological values, which require theology to engage in a self-aware contextuality.[17] Theology conducted from a place of privilege will often display the blindnesses and biases of that position, and often promote (wittingly or unwittingly) the interests of those with privilege. Cone recognizes his own theological limitations and the particularity of his formation. He claims about the Black church in which he grew up, "It was the world I grew up in. My identity as a human being comes out of the church."[18] And so does his theology. And so does all of ours; it arises from the social context in which we have been formed and trained—the stories that have shaped our lives and our way of life, the history and stories of our various denominations or congregations, our sins and struggles.

Ethics as Formation

At this point, we can return to where we started: Bonhoeffer and the formation of ministers and other Christian leaders. Bonhoeffer outlines his view of Christian formation in an underappreciated essay that appears to have been intended as the Introduction to his book on *Ethics*, titled "Ethics as Formation." That book was never completed, interrupted by his arrest, but fragments remain, and I will highlight some of the most interesting things he writes in that short essay—written several years after the closing of Finkenwalde, but perhaps reflecting upon that experiment in theological formation.

Bonhoeffer's account of formation stands on three legs: Christology, church, and context. Bonhoeffer begins by turning to the person and work of Christ as the content of formation. Rather than principles or programs, Bonhoeffer says that theology should not be built on such abstract concepts but upon the living God—and specifically the image of the crucified Christ.[19] It is from Jesus Christ, the Reconciler who steps in between the sin of the world and the holiness of God, that "proceeds all the formation of a world reconciled with God."[20] That is, "Formation occurs only by being drawn into the form of Jesus Christ, by being conformed to the unique form of the one who became human, was crucified, and is risen." This occurs as the form of Jesus Christ molds the community and conforms our form to Christ's own.[21] This reflects the coupling of faith and obedience that Bonhoeffer described in *Discipleship*—insisting that "only the believers obey, and only the obedient believe"[22]—and that frames his emphasis on costly grace that has animated theologians and practitioners as divergent as James Dobson and James Cone. Christ is the human being for others, and as Christians become conformed to his likeness, they also become humans "for others." Lisa Dahill notes, "to the extent that Christians participate in [Christ's] form, being conformed to him, they too take on the role of *Stellverter* [vicarious representative] of others and of Christ in the world."[23] And as Karen Guth adds, Bonhoeffer's notions of vicarious representation and "being for others" are not simply calls to self-sacrifice, but—important for those of us in privileged positions—better understood as "conditions of solidarity with the other."[24]

Second, Bonhoeffer not only proposes the content for formation but also its methodology. As Dahill observes, "For him, there can be no solitary formation; the life of the church is constitutive of the Christian."[25] In other words, formation occurs through the practices of the church.[26] In *Sanctorum Communio*, Bonhoeffer speaks of the church as breaking into the world and disrupting the ordinary rhythm of life, as the form of Christ in the world.[27] And later in *Ethics*, the church breaks into the world specifically as the cruciform Body of Christ—bearing the guilt of the sin of the world, for the sake of the world. As he famously claims in *Ethics*, the Christian is called to the *responsible life*, which consists of (1) vicarious representative action on behalf of others and (2) acting in accordance with reality, that is, with full attention to the concrete context and situation one finds oneself.[28] This is Christological action, and thus ecclesiological action: the practices and disciplines of the church—time together and alone, in prayer or in work—train us to stand with and for the other like Christ, in the place where the other lives, becoming vulnerable to what they are vulnerable to, risking what they risk, whatever challenges or struggles they confront. This means, for Bonhoeffer, all ethics and all theology necessarily begins in ecclesiology—in the ways we inhabit and are shaped by the church.

Finally, Bonhoeffer concludes that this form of Christ takes shape in *real, concrete* human beings, "and thus in quite different ways" in their own contexts. This is no one-size-fits-all formation. Universal ethical programs lead only to abstraction and remove us from the concrete embodiment of the ethical action to which Christ calls us. As Townes suggests of womanism, the heart of ethics is the "self-other relation grounded in concrete existence."[29] The concrete Christian ethic, on the other hand, means that "we can and should speak not about what the good is, can be, or should be for each and every time, but about *how Christ may take form among us today and here.*"[30] The question of how Christ takes form among us today, and how we can be conformed to him, is impossible to determine for all times and places. We must, Bonhoeffer later says, attend to the "particular context of experience, responsibility, and decision, from which we cannot withdraw without ending up in abstraction."[31] Christ forms us in a concrete manner to act in accordance with the particular, worldly, and public reality in which we find ourselves. It is in "life's duties, problems, success and failures, experiences and perplexities" that we are formed, he says. And in the particularities of our context, we are formed to see the sufferings of our neighbors.[32]

And this sets up the argument that privileged Christians have a contextualized, situated ethic, one shaped by our particular social location and formation. In my previous book, *Witnessing Whiteness*, I argued that white Christians had a special responsibility for the racial harms perpetrated in Christianity's name—even for the origins of white supremacy itself. In that book, I proposed an ethic of responsibility that stood on the practical pillars of remembrance, repentance, and reparations.[33] I think the same is true for privileged Christians. We are the ones who have historically controlled the way Christianity was interpreted and employed, and thus we bear the responsibility for its global harms. But more on that to come.

Understanding the task of Christian ethics as a contextual work of formation into a life of discipleship shaped by one's community, social location, and experiences is the first step in building a Christian ethics for privileged people. It is only by first understanding the nature of ethical reflection and reckoning with one's own position of privilege and poverty (and the histories that rendered that position) that we can begin to properly understand the resources we need to develop a liberatory ethic. That is the task for Chapter 2. There we turn to the models and sources of Christian ethics. It provides a framework for the argument outlined in this chapter and analyzes how these methods and sources shape the contextualized, formative approach of the book.

Epilogue

The Gestapo shut down Finkenwalde seminary in the summer of 1937. Yet, Bonhoeffer continued pursuing the "superior discipline" of ethical formation to the very end. On the morning of April 8, 1945, he led an Easter worship service for a group of prisoners who had spent the night in an abandoned schoolhouse in Bavaria. They were being transported to Flossenburg concentration camp. Bonhoeffer had spent time as a pastor, a youth minister, a theology student, a university professor, and the founder of an underground seminary when all churches were required to swear an oath of allegiance to Hitler. But now Bonhoeffer was simply a prisoner. He had spent the past two years in an assortment of jails, prisons, and labor camps and was eventually charged with engaging in a conspiracy to assassinate Hitler. That morning, he read from 1 Pet. 1:3: "Blessed be the God and Father of our Lord Jesus Christ! According to his great mercy he has caused us to be born again to a living hope through the resurrection of Jesus Christ from the dead."[34] The next morning, Bonhoeffer was taken from his cell, led to the gallows, and hanged—two weeks before American soldiers liberated the camp.

He wrote that the church is the presence of God in the world and is often called the church, "Christ existing as community"—the literal Body of Christ, hands and feet working in the world on behalf of its redemption, even when you cannot see or feel it, even when that Body appears hanging and nailed to a tree. Even in some of his last writings and last words, he proclaimed the church as our living hope, often appearing to be broken, useless, and lifeless, but always brought back to life, forming us through the resurrection of Jesus Christ from the dead for the salvation of the world.

To understand Christian ethics as formation, with a primary focus on witness and context, is to recognize the social conditioning of that formation—from the early church to the church of the enslaved to the white denominations that have continually neglected any social responsibility. It is to recognize witness not only as a positive moral example but also as confession, repentance, repair, and forgiveness. So, as we turn now to the methods of doing Christian ethics and its primary sources of authority, Cone and Cannon, Bonhoeffer and the *Didache*, all teach us to proceed humbly—recognizing our finitude and limitations, that our ethical witness must first be one of confession and caution—as we discern together within and across our contexts what it means to follow Christ.

Notes

1 Christiane Tietz, *Theologian of Resistance: The Life and Thought of Dietrich Bonhoeffer*, trans. V. Barnett (Minneapolis, MN: Fortress Press, 2016), 59.

2 This quote and anecdote come from Charles Marsh, *Strange Glory: A Life of Dietrich Bonhoeffer* (New York: Alfred A. Knopf, 2014), 257.

3 Dietrich Bonhoeffer, *Life Together, Dietrich Bonhoeffer Works (English)*, vol. 5, ed. Geffrey B. Kelly, trans. Daniel W. Bloesch and James H. Burtness (Minneapolis, MN: Fortress Press, 1996), 27.

4 Geffrey Kelley and F. Burton Nelson, *The Cost of Moral Leadership: The Spirituality of Dietrich Bonhoeffer* (Grand Rapids, MI: Eerdmans Publishing, 2003), 158.

5 Katie G. Cannon, *Black Womanist Ethics* (Atlanta, GA: Scholars Press, 1988), 2–3.

6 Cannon, 75.

7 Cannon, 75.

8   Dietrich Bonhoeffer, *Sanctorum Communio, Dietrich Bonhoeffer Works (English)*, vol. 1, ed. Clifford Green, trans. Reinhard Krauss and Nancy Lukens (Minneapolis, MN: Fortress Press, 1998), 51, 48.
9   Bonhoeffer, *Sanctorum Communio*, DBWE 1, 49.
10 Dietrich Bonhoeffer, "What Is Meant by 'Telling the Truth?'" in *Ethics*, ed. Eberhard. Bethge (New York: Touchstone, 1995), 358–68.
11 Stacey Floyd-Thomas, *Mining the Motherlode: Methods in Womanist Ethics* (Cleveland, OH: Pilgrim Press, 2006), 34.
12 Howard Selsam, *Socialism and Ethics* (New York: International Publishers, 1943), 17.
13 James Cone, *God of the Oppressed* (Maryknoll, NY: Orbis Books, 1973), 40, 38.
14 James Cone, *For My People* (Maryknoll, NY: Orbis Books, 1986), 148; quoting Gustavo Gutiérrez, *The Power of the Poor in History* (Maryknoll, NY: Orbis Books, 1983), 90–1.
15 Emilie Townes, *Womanist Ethics and the Cultural Production of Evil* (New York: Palgrave MacMillan, 2007), 12, 113.
16 James Cone, "Christian Faith and Political Praxis," *Encounter* 43, no. 2 (1982): 129–41, 130.
17 Townes, 113.
18 Cone interview with author, April 12, 2016, in New York.
19 Dietrich Bonhoeffer, *Ethics, Dietrich Bonhoeffer Works (English)*, vol. 6, ed. Clifford Green, trans. Reinhard Krauss, Charles C. West, and Douglas W. Stott (Minneapolis, MN: Fortress Press, 2005), 81.
20 Bonhoeffer, *Ethics*, DBWE 6, 92.
21 Bonhoeffer, *Ethics*, DBWE 6, 93. Here, Bonhoeffer cites Gal. 4:9.
22 Dietrich Bonhoeffer, *Discipleship, Dietrich Bonhoeffer Works (English)*, vol. 4, ed. John Godsey and Geffrey B. Kelly, trans. Reinhard Krauss and Barbara Green (Minneapolis, MN: Fortress Press, 2003), 63.
23 Lisa Dahill, *Reading from the Underside of Selfhood: Bonhoeffer and Spiritual Formation* (Eugene, OR: Pickwick Publications, 2009), 188.
24 Karen V. Guth, "To See From Below: Dietrich Bonhoeffer's Mandates and Feminist Ethics," *Journal of the Society of Christian Ethics* 33, no. 2 (2013): 131–50, 142.
25 Dahill, 106.

26 Bonhoeffer, *Ethics*, DBWE 6, 96.
27 I discuss this in more detail in "The Incarnational Church: Bonhoeffer's Political Ecclesiology of Transformation," in *A Spoke in the Wheel: The Political in the Theology of Dietrich Bonhoeffer*, ed. K. Busch Nielson, Ralf K. Wustenberg, and Jen Zimmermann (Munich: Gütersloher Verlagshaus, 2013), 325–38. Ralf K, Wüstenberg, Jen Zimmermann
28 Bonhoeffer, *Ethics*, DBWE 6, 257–60.
29 Emilie Townes, "To Be Called Beloved: Womanist Ontology in Postmodern Refraction," in *Womanist Theological Ethics*, ed. Katie Geneva Cannon, Emilie Townes, and Angela Sims (Louisville, KY: Westminster John Knox Press, 2011), 200.
30 Bonhoeffer, *Ethics*, DBWE 6, 99.
31 Bonhoeffer, *Ethics*, DBWE 6, 101.
32 Dietrich Bonhoeffer, *Letters and Papers from Prison, DBWE* 8, ed. John W. de Gruchy, trans. Isabel Best, Lisa E. Dahill, Reinhard Krauss, and Nancy Lukens (Minneapolis, MN: Fortress Press, 2010), 542.
33 Kristopher Norris, *Witnessing Whiteness: Confronting White Supremacy in the American Church* (Oxford, UK: Oxford University Press, 2020).
34 Eberhard Bethge, *Dietrich Bonhoeffer: A Biography* (rev. ed.), ed. V. Barnett (Minneapolis, MN: Fortress Press, 2000), 926–7.

2

Models and Sources

Introduction: *The Good Place*

Being ethical is not easy.

Pop culture does not often explore the deep recesses of moral philosophy, but the popular 2010s sitcom *The Good Place* ventured to do so. Through four seasons, this show, created by Michael Schur—of *The Office* and *Parks and Recreation* fame—followed four individuals who had died and believed themselves to be in "the good place." During their various misadventures to uncover their true whereabouts, they encountered Douglas Ewing, formerly of Scaggsville, Maryland, who gave his mother a dozen roses and lost moral points in the afterlife's comically archaic point system by doing so.

Why would such a generous and loving act generate negative points and leave the giver in the not-so-good place? The viewer quickly learns that the flowers were ordered using a cell phone made in a sweatshop, picked by exploited migrant workers, grown with toxic pesticides, delivered from thousands of miles away through a process rendering a significant carbon footprint, and profiting a racist CEO with a penchant for sending unwanted photographs to his female employees. As one character exclaims, "Everyday the world gets a little more complicated and being a good person becomes harder."[1]

I recall watching this episode as a graduate student in ethics and thinking, perhaps our world has rendered every action morally ambiguous. Not only is it impossible to know the thousand moral implications and consequences of every action, but trying to align ethical rules and goals within this complex framework is a fool's errand.[2] One of the main characters in the show is Chidi Anagonye, a moral philosopher, who, finding himself (spoiler alert!) also not in the actual Good Place after a lifetime of ethical learning and realizing the impossibility of acting ethically, descends into a fit of nihilism during which he cooks a pot of Peeps chili and tells a classroom of students that moral theories are "hot stinking cat dookie." (Maybe you should just watch it for yourself.) Still, as he regains his wits and attempts to teach a fellow lost soul how to be moral, he offers an overview of the most significant threads of moral philosophy, which also correspond to the traditional models of Christian ethics. I'll provide a brief, less comical outline of them.

Conventional Models of Christian Ethics

When scholars talk about Christian ethics today, they often divide the field into three prominent categories—three frameworks in which to think about the Christian moral life. These align with the three most prominent categories of philosophical ethics, a point that both speaks to the way Christian ethics has been shaped by external (secular) sources and to their centrality within the practice of the Christian moral life. These three themes are duty, results, and character.

I imagine that we all operate in our everyday lives with a mixture of these ethical methods—sometimes leaning on one, sometimes on another, without thinking much about it. I imagine this is true even if we think we prefer one framework over another. This reality makes it even more important to think about them theoretically so that we will be aware of the times we are acting consistently and why we may prefer one method over another.

Duty / Deontology

An ethical commitment to duty is what moral philosophers call deontological ethics. Deontology revolves around a responsibility to something outside of the self, a set of universal rules, and focuses on motive instead of the objective or end of one's action. Morality is expressed in terms of *imperatives, rules,* and *duties.* We do certain things for the sake of duty, not because they lead to certain results and not because of what they do to us as agents.

One popular example of this approach is represented by the philosopher Immanuel Kant. Kant's ethical model revolves around a moral obligation, the idea of a law to which all rational beings are subject. Kant called this universal principle of practical reasoning the Categorical Imperative, which is this: "Always act in such a way that you would will your action to be a universal law for all humanity." In other words, an action is moral for Kant if you would wish that everyone acted that way. This means that an action is not judged by its results, but by its intention, whether one follows the rule. In fact, Kant considered this a universalized conception of the "golden rule:" Do unto others as you wish everyone in the world to also do.

Likewise, a deontological view of Christian ethics maintains that Christian morality consists primarily of fulfilling our divinely given duties to others or obeying God's *commands*—"go and do likewise." It is doing good works because God commands us to do so. We owe obligations to one another, and we do this because God tells us so. If you watched *The Good Place*, Chidi operated primarily from a deontological perspective—what do we owe one another? For another example, let's look at one of the most famous ethical teachings in the Gospels, one of Jesus' sayings in the Sermon on the Mount.

Jesus said

> You have heard that it was said, "You shall love your neighbor and hate your enemy." But I say to you, "Love your enemies and pray for those who persecute you, so that you may be children of your Father in heaven; for he makes his sun rise on the evil and on the good, and sends rain on the righteous and on the unrighteous. For if you love those who love you, what reward do you have?" (Mt. 5:43-46)

Deontologists would understand this story in terms of an imperative—Christians are to love their enemies because they are commanded by Jesus to do so. Jesus seems to be saying that this is how human beings are to treat one another—it is our duty to love one another whether that other is a neighbor or an enemy. Loving those who love you is an easy obligation, but loving an enemy goes above and beyond—and this serves as a universal imperative because we would like our enemies to treat us in the same way.

Results / Consequentialism

The second framework is based on results or outcomes. A consequentialist ethical approach says that right and wrong can only be assessed by the goodness of the *consequences*, the *ends* that one is aiming to achieve. We engage in an action because it will bring about a moral end or the greatest good.

One of the most prominent examples of this is utilitarianism, promoted by philosophers John Stuart Mill and Jeremy Bentham. This states, "An act is right if, of those choices available to the agent at the time, this particular act would produce the greatest overall value." Mill argues that actions are right in proportion to the degree they promote happiness and wrong to the degree they produce the reverse of happiness. Happiness is the ultimate *goal* or consequence we want to achieve, so we should seek actions that make the greatest number of people happy or pleased. Whatever creates the greatest happiness for the greatest number of people is the moral thing to do.

In this way, a Christian consequentialism says that we can judge the rightness of an action based on the effect or outcome it produces. Christian actions are moral insofar as they produce good consequences. Christian ethics consists of actions that lead to good results. The great Christian ethicist Reinhold Niebuhr understood that this sometimes meant choosing between two or more less-than-ideal options (choosing the lesser of two evils). His Christian Realism approach to ethics was a form of consequentialism. For example, he famously justified the dropping of the atomic bomb in 1945.[3] His rationale for doing so was that the number of lives it eventually saved by ending the war immediately outnumbered the lives that were lost in the bombing. (At the risk of becoming an advertisement for the show, you might check out *The Good Place's* episode dedicated to the Trolley Problem, the most prominent thought experiment of consequentialism [Season 2, Episode 6].)

So, let's look at our Sermon on the Mount example of loving enemies. A consequentialist would say that Jesus is telling us to do this because, in the end, loving enemies leads to a better and more peaceful society—and that is the goal. In the immediate future it may lead to disaster, weakness, and even being taken advantage of by others who do not live by such a code (as Luther would argue). It doesn't make sense as an expedient social and political policy—as Niebuhr points out. But a consequentialist who takes the long view may conclude that, as evidence suggests that nonviolent methods achieve a group's goals more effectively than violent ones (see Chapter 5), the results are ultimately good and beautiful, with society eventually becoming more peaceful and stable.

Character / Virtue Ethics

The final framework of virtue ethics is concerned with the question, "What is the highest good in life?" and then the development of a person or community's character around that good. Virtue ethicists evaluate actions in terms of the type of character one should strive to cultivate through those actions. For example, if a community's highest good or character trait (called a virtue) is accumulating money, then they would evaluate every decision by the criterion of whether it would form them into the type of person who would make more money. If it is the overall health of humanity, actions would be evaluated in terms of how healthy it makes the people of the world.

A prime proponent of virtue ethics is Aristotle, who understood ethics in terms of the question "What is the chief good for humans?" or "What is ultimately worth aiming at?" Morality, in this model, is based on the ultimate purpose and character of humans. Aristotle says that only virtue is sufficient as the final ultimate end of human existence.

What does this mean for Christian ethics? First, we need to define virtue. Virtue, for Aristotle, is "human excellence that can be realized in distinctively human (rational) activity." This means, importantly, that virtue is realized in practice, by engaging in activities over a period of time. Second, how do we acquire virtues? Through *habituation*, or training; we are not born with them. We can't decide simply to be virtuous in a singular event or situation; we have to learn how to be virtuous from training and watching exemplary people. In this way, developing virtues follows the same process as learning to play an instrument or play a sport. It takes practice. Melanie Harris helpfully develops a virtue framework for a womanist ethic, again, from the perspective of Black women concerned with the intersecting injustices of patriarchy and racism. She defines virtue as "a disposition or characteristic habitually developed over time in the individual and in the community that marks good moral character and reflects certain basic values, such as wholeness and good community." Her definition reflects the ultimate good of wholeness or good community and suggests the need to develop character to achieve that good over time. She adds, "Virtues *practiced habitually* through everyday actions and behaviors influence the way ethical decisions are made."[4]

Again, turning to our Sermon on the Mount example: a Christian virtue ethicist understands Jesus to be giving an example of a practice that develops virtue. Practices like loving enemies and not simply neighbors make us into better people. Repeatedly trying to love enemies is an activity that cultivates the type of character that points to our highest purposes as Christians (loving God and others as ourselves), no matter what happens to us, no matter whether this community is totally overrun by a violent mob (as in Luther's concern). Practicing love of enemy creates a people with the virtues necessary to care for one another in imitation of Jesus. This is even suggested in the Gospel passage. Jesus goes on to say at the conclusion of this exhortation, "Be perfect, therefore, as your heavenly Father is perfect" (5:48). This suggests that practicing enemy love creates perfection. It is not an end unto itself—a rule to follow or a calculated action based on a desired outcome. It is a step in a process of one's formation into the character of God.

I will develop this analysis more at the end of this chapter, but before turning to the resources that inform this ethical model, let me add another word on the importance of context. As I said at the outset of this chapter, most of us likely flit through all three of these frameworks without thinking much about them. The models do not always need to be in conflict; as some moral philosophers point out, the various schools of thought are akin to mountaineers "climbing the same mountain on different sides."[5] However, it would also be a mistake to reduce Christian ethics to these three categories, or to think that they exist abstractly above the context in which we reason ethically. They help us to make critical sense of ethics but should not determine ethics—that is, Christian ethics resides within, above, and beyond these three categories. As we learned in the Chapter 1, the contextual nature of Christian ethics is more complex than any individual model.

Sources for Christian Ethics

These three models for considering how to act morally do not stand alone. Any framework necessarily relies upon various sources to provide material content for the model. To what sources will one turn when considering what action will lead to the best outcome or what practices will shape a virtuous character? One conventional way of thinking about ethical sources is with the "quadrilateral" of sources for theology. These four items resource a person or a community's theological framework, while of course, some give more weight to one or another source. They are scripture, tradition, reason, and experience.

But before developing each a little more closely, I want to return to James Cone to help us understand how to think about ethical "sources" from a liberationist perspective. Cone emphasizes the importance of social context. Yet, context cannot simply determine our ethics; there is more to ethical reasoning than simply our social conditioning. So, we must turn to other sources—and he calls these sources *witnesses*. The Bible, Christian tradition, experience: these are all *witnesses* to the Gospel of Christ. And, again, I think this is a helpful framing because it properly identifies these conventional sources. None is sufficient for moral reasoning, none is determinative, and they each point toward something greater than itself. Like witnesses, they each provide one part of a whole story. Some may give more relevant information in one moral situation than another, but taken together, they allow us to piece together all the resources necessary to think and act ethically. Let's start with scripture.

Scripture

According to 2 Tim. 3:16, all scripture is inspired, or *God-breathed*, and useful for teaching. Jesus referred back to the Hebrew scriptures to shape his teachings. We may all recall from Christian History class that the Protestant Reformation was a "back to the Bible" movement that made scripture—and every individual's interpretation of it—the central source for conducting one's life. *Sola scriptura* ("Scripture alone"), a central tenet of the Reformation, is a claim about authority. For many Protestant churches, Scripture became the sole true authority by which every claim must be tested. (As the Southern Baptist pastors from my upbringing liked to insist: there is no creed but the Bible!) Faithfulness to Scripture became the sole criterion for determining the authority of any religious official or authority. In fact, as soon as he was excommunicated from the Roman Catholic Church and went into hiding, Martin Luther spent that year completing the first translation of the Bible into German so that the masses would have unmediated access to this sole authority.

In Christian circles, we often hear people ask, "What does the Bible say about that?" Growing up in conservative circles during debates over human sexuality, I would often hear the phrase "biblical view of marriage" imposed as a conversation stopper, as if there were one singular model of marriage in the Bible. But the difficulty with scripture is that it is often not straightforward in its guidance. We have to remember that the Bible was a document written in particular contexts—that means it is also shaped by the cultural contexts of its writers. It was written over hundreds of years by many different authors living in different times, circumstances, and addressing different audiences, and containing different literary genres from poetry to historical prose to symbolic prophecy to parables. And then you have the problem of translating these texts from Greek, Hebrew, and Aramaic into English or another language. Often the Bible gives unclear advice, and even seems to advocate conflicting positions: Jesus says in the gospels that he has both come to bring peace and come to bring the sword (Jn 14:27, Mt. 10:34). Well, which one is it, Jesus?

Despite this, the Bible has been the most important factor in determining what it means to be a Christian and how Christians should behave. But this does take us back to the problem of *context*. Our contexts are lenses through which we interpret the Bible, which is why Cone calls the Bible a *witness*. We each approach a biblical text already fitted with a background of experiences, beliefs, and expectations that will filter our interpretation of that text. How we read and interpret it will be shaped and even determined by our place and time, our social status, and other ideological commitments.

Therefore, we must place the Bible, the other sources (especially experience), and our context in a dialectical relationship. And we must be humble about our moral conclusions.

Tradition

Christian tradition typically includes the development of the history, creeds, teachings, worship, prayers, and hymns of the church community through its 2,000-year history. Christian ethics is not an individual enterprise. In fact, Christians have historically been suspicious of individuals interpreting right action or belief on their own—until the Reformation and the contemporary dominant influence of American individualism. Christian ethics is a communal work, done as part of a long tradition and community that spans both globe and generation. The churches of the Reformation generally adopted church traditions—including infant baptism and the doctrine of the Trinity—if they were justified by scripture and had been articulated during the early history of the church.

Tradition is valuable for ethical reflection because it takes into account the context in which the ethical work is being done. It amplifies the history and thoughts of scholars, monastics, martyrs, and witnesses from the past, as well as the present context. Tradition takes into account the practically formative elements of morality (such as denominations, worship styles, rituals, and liturgy) as well as the importance of the community in moral discernment. It doesn't just leave all moral discernment up to "you and the Bible" and whatever you think it says, but includes the entire community—most often a church—into the moral development of a people. It helpfully turns the priesthood of THE believer into the priesthood of ALL believers (in community and throughout history).

Here again, Cone views tradition as a witness. He says that it "opens our story of Christ to other stories in the past and thus forces us to move outside the subjectivity of our present."[6] We must understand the social and political conditioning of tradition: there have been winners and losers in the Christian tradition, and thus we must also be able to critique it. The Christian tradition has supported slavery and genocide, empire and oppression, and we must not neglect the bad for the good, but learn from our failures.

Tradition is the great cloud of witnesses of Christianity's past, and not just from orthodox or European contexts but from a variety of cultures—the witness of underrepresented and forgotten voices as well. And Cone would say that the ethical source of "tradition" compels us to seek out these neglected voices and prioritize their witness.

Reason

The third witness is reason. This is the driving force behind the three moral philosophies we investigated: Kant's categorical imperative, Mill's utilitarianism, and Aristotle's virtue. All three of these approaches are predicated upon what the rational mind thinks is the most effective, productive, and healthy action. Reason has historically been the foundation for moral reflection and is an essential ingredient in Christian ethics as well. In a Christian context, reason helps us to sift through scripture and tradition in an attempt to make a coherent ethical system out of it.

Reason helps a person to move through and past contexts—as best we can—to take scripture, written in a completely different context, and think about how it might apply today. It also takes into account scientific truth—what has changed in what we know: Earth is not flat; it revolves around the sun. Sometimes it conflicts: people don't rise from the dead; they don't walk on water. Sometimes it challenges: how do we square the creation story and that of the flood with what we know about evolution?

In the end, though, we must always remember a few caveats. First, reason is not universal—it is bound to the traditions and experiences of different contexts. What is deemed reasonable within one community and context may not be reasonable within another. We should be suspicious of any pretensions to reason alone or a universalized sense of rationality. Second, Christians must also acknowledge sinfulness and how that hinders our rational mind, as well as what reason tells us. As the Apostle Paul says, we can only "see through a glass darkly" (1 Cor. 13:12). And third, as Cone reminds us, reason has often been the champion of oppression—it has been associated with white European intellectualism and has been used to degrade other cultures as unreasonable or unintelligent and often used to separate theology from just ethical action. So, we must approach and appeal to reason with caution.

Experience

Finally, experience considers a person or community's past and outside influences. Including experience as a fourth source both acknowledges that one's context serves as a filter for all the other sources and also serves as an ethical source itself.

Often in Christian history, experience has been used to counter oppressive traditions (like slavery or the oppression of women). It asks, "How do the experiences of you and your community impact how you think morally?" Recall from Chapter 1 Katie Cannon's argument that enslaved people developed their own ethical code that was radically different from what their oppressors taught them. Her model of virtue ethics, as any concerned with a person or community's context, begins by considering one's experience.

Experience also raises the issues of pluralism, objectivity (can a person be completely unbiased), and personal context. It doesn't mean that anything goes or that something is morally right simply because you feel it is right or your own context suggests it is right. Experience cannot stand as a source without including critical reflection on our own experiences. But our individual and communal experiences and contexts are inescapable and are bound to influence the way we interpret scripture, understand our tradition (and to which tradition we belong), and inflect our reason. The Reformation, which in generalized terms was suspicious of experience as a theological and ethical source, helped develop and distinguish the spiritual from the secular. Cone, from his liberationist perspective, does not see a great distinction between secular and sacred.[7] The sacred can be discovered in the blues music emanating from a rowdy juke joint in the Jim Crow South—or in a sunset, a newspaper article, philosophical text, or scientific discovery. As the Psalmist sings, all of creation declares the glory of God. "There is no language where their voice is not heard" (19:3). For Cone, all of experience can be sacred and a source for Christian ethical thinking. Our experiences of culture, entertainment, literature, and encounters with other religions can all helpfully shape our morality.

Putting It All Together

This discussion leads to the question of how to prioritize or rank these sources of moral thought. Again, for Cone, the validity of any ethical claim resides in the authority of Christ. Christ is the adjudicator, measure, and judge of these sources for Christian ethics. He says, drawing on Bonhoeffer, that we must ask: Who is Jesus Christ for us today? Does a specific claim or action conform to who Christ is? But importantly, for him, who Jesus Christ is today is not an open-ended question that can be filled with just any content or constructed in our own image. Rather, that question must be answered by looking at who Jesus *was*—the historical Jesus. Jesus was an oppressed Jew who died at the hands of Empire and religious authorities, who proclaimed freedom to the captive and poor and came to liberate the oppressed. Any answer to the question of who Christ is or what Christ is up to in the world—and therefore any answer to the ethical question of how we are to follow Christ in the world—must conform to this liberating historical Jesus. And so, Cone says that any measure of these sources, or witnesses, must point to God's universal will to liberate humanity, and especially those who are oppressed. Following Jesus dictates a life led to liberate others from oppression and, in doing so, liberating ourselves. These four witnesses guide the way.

Why Virtue?

Now that the primary models and sources of Christian ethics have been laid out, you may be asking—why virtue? As I noted in the introduction, this book offers an argument for a communitarian *virtue* ethic of liberation. But why does the witness of these sources and the reality of our constant shifting between moral theories in practice lead me to commend virtue ethics as the path most likely to lead to liberation? I admit, you don't find many activists or liberation scholars who are primarily concerned with achieving just results advocating for an ethics of character development in order to get there. Virtue ethics, with its traditional focus on the inward cultivation of an individual's own moral goodness, has not often been associated with the revolutionary acts of liberation. Yet, I believe there is a natural affinity between the small, integral work of cultivating goodness through habits of character development and achieving communities of wholeness, responsibility, and justice. A few scholars and a television show may help my case.

Back to *The Good Place* (you could have guessed). Throughout his life and afterlife, Chidi struggles to reconcile his ethical training with his journey to earn his way into the actual Good Place. His driving moral question is to ask "what we owe to each other?" an explicit reference to a book by ethicist Tim Scanlon, and a full promotion of the duty-oriented approach of deontology. Yet, as Chidi gradually gains awareness of the moral complexity of the world (and afterworld) and the reality that even following universally rational rules can lead to negative consequences—like in the example of Douglas Ewing—Chidi and the series in general gradually begin embracing virtue ethics, or at least holding the two models together. In a world of moral uncertainty, ethical theories that assume you can predictably calculate results or propose universal rules across contexts fall short. As one commentator notes, "Many moral theories take a somewhat Yoda-ish approach.... You abide by a set of reasonable rules, or you don't; you maximize the good in the world, or you don't—there is no try." But in a morally ambiguous world, a truly realistic approach understands that the best we might be capable of accomplishing in many situations is to *try*. And, as the showrunner notes, "By focusing on cultivating virtues, on personal growth and development, an Aristotelian [virtue] approach puts trying front and center."[8] So, my first argument is that virtue provides the best ethical model for a world of moral ambiguity.

But what of its inward, individualist focus? Even Aristotle acknowledged that not all virtues were directed toward inward fulfillment: "[T]hose qualities are noble which give more pleasure to other people than to their possessors," and "the best man is not he who exercises his excellence toward himself but he who exercises it towards another."[9] Aristotle believed that by acting virtuously toward others, the virtuous agent would receive benefit in some form. This reflects Martin Luther King's "No one is free until all are free" maxim or an African *ubuntu* sentiment: "I am who I am because you are who you are." The interdependence of all humans in a community means that the good life for everyone is necessary for any one person's well-being. (Though, Aristotle is not sufficient here since he did not believe everyone [i.e., women and slaves] belonged to a political community equally.) Based on a belief in interconnectivity—a key component of womanist theology—virtue can be a communal practice, focused outwardly on how the character of the community receives and responds to others. So secondly, a virtue ethic of liberation seeks practices that will cultivate the character of an entire community as responding to others, not simply individuals within the community. (I'll note that herein lie similarities to the communalism of Stanley Hauerwas and postliberal virtue theory, but I'll address that more directly in Chapter 3.)

The communal focus of virtue ethics also brings us back to the issue of contextuality. As Katie Cannon observes, "Any canonical virtues or values that are part of a community are indeed shaped by the cultural context and experiences of that community."[10] Womanist theologian Melanie Harris argues that Cannon actually developed a womanist *virtue* ethic by utilizing an *inductive* approach that examined cultural circumstances at the beginning of its moral deliberation. This womanist virtue ethic centers the experience and voices of the community, as well as the witness of those outside of the community speaking to it and holding it accountable. Harris further leans on Cannon's womanist ethical method to explicitly develop a methodology for a womanist virtue ethic. Remember her definition of virtue within this womanist framework: "a disposition or characteristic habitually developed over time in the individual *and* in the community that marks good moral character and reflects certain basic values, such as wholeness and good community." As we will discuss in Chapter 3, she notes, "Virtues practiced habitually through everyday actions and behaviors influence the way ethical decisions are made."[11] This model starts with experience and lifts up "experiential themes" from the real life of the community. It then highlights ethical implications within that experience and gleans moral virtues from those implications.[12] For example, Harris draws on the work of Alice Walker, using her literature to illustrate the experience of Black women. From this, she begins with Walker's "experiential theme" of fragmentation due to segregation internalized within Black women's bodies. This theme leads to the ethical implication of equity and then the virtue of wholeness.[13]

So, thus far, virtue ethics is (1) the best guide to navigate moral uncertainty, and (2) it focuses on community and context. But can it ultimately lead to justice and liberation, especially regarding privileged Christians? Lisa Tessman, a feminist scholar writing about virtue within marginalized communities, argues that a virtue framework is important for thinking about justice and liberation because other moral theories overlook the limitations of the Self, or the community, in achieving moral goods by racing toward ends or results. While acknowledging limitations, virtue ethics in a liberatory register still recognizes that developing a good character is a necessary part of making the good life accessible for all.[14] While oppressed communities do not have the freedom to always exercise full moral agency, she believes that virtue ethics can help any community think about what it means to be morally good and engage in morally good behaviors even in a position it did not explicitly choose. She calls these "burdened virtues"—meaning they are the best one can offer in a particular circumstance but leave a moral remainder.[15]

Just as being subject to oppression influences one's chances of developing a good character, as Tessman argues, so does being enmeshed in social privilege. While the oppressed are clearly denied certain external, material factors important for flourishing, the character of the privileged is also negatively impacted by vices and the absence of certain virtues conditioned by their location. A communal virtue ethic for privileged people may require uncovering, interrogating, and changing aspects of one's character developed under conditions of privilege once one begins to understand them as harmful. If systemic issues significantly impact the responsibility one has for the development of their own character as well as the forward-looking responsibility they have toward others, then, Tessman argues, a liberatory ethical theory can only address that responsibility by focusing on character or virtue. By centering character, a person or community can begin identifying how to develop the virtues necessary to carry out the actions needed for liberation.[16]

Thus, drawing on Tessman's prescription for a feminist virtue ethics, we might say a communitarian virtue ethics for privileged people examines systemic barriers to liberation and flourishing created by oppression by asking what virtues need to be developed in order to challenge those barriers and resist further formation by privilege, while recognizing that some conditions and social formations are beyond our control. There are limits to our agency and our ability to develop good character. Still, we must not eschew responsibility.

A brief interlude on terms, here: When I talk about "privileged people" in this book, I am not speaking about those who intentionally and wickedly exploit vices in order to impose violence on others and maintain their positions of privilege—the health insurance CEO or sweatshop owner. But, following Tessman, I am speaking more generally about those with "ordinary" privileges like a hardworking middle-class family who resists economic redistribution policies, or the white family who believes in colorblindness and lives in a gated community. I mean those who maintain themselves in unjust social locations or simply uncritically accept the conditions of their privilege. Privileged people are "structurally enabled to think of themselves as good and to think of their lives as happy lives" because they may simply not notice the suffering of others or at least do not understand a causal relationship between the others' suffering and their own privilege.[17] For example, the segregated nature of our residential lives prohibits privileged white people from seeing the unjust daily realities of those who live in predominantly Black neighborhoods.

A highway cuts through the middle of my home city, dividing it racially. Unless I intentionally choose to live in or drive to that part of town, where there are fewer grocery stores, banks, businesses, and parks, I am blinded to the everyday realities of what my privileged livelihood is rendering to others. So, this also includes those of us—including myself—born into economically and socially privileged positions who are struggling with how to use that privilege to make a difference in the world. We experience barriers to virtue, especially impediments to "other-regarding" virtues or the direction of other-regarding virtues only to others who are also privileged, due to our practices of or involuntary participation in practices of domination. The privileged experience "burdened" virtues as well.

For the privileged, character leads to responsibility. A virtue ethic is linked with an ethic of responsibility: as a community engages in practices that become habits that produce good moral character, that community becomes more aware of its own moral shortcomings as well as the ways its behaviors are linked to others—interconnectivity. For Harris, a womanist approach to virtue ethics includes three aspects of responsibility.[18]

First is responsibility as *mutual relationality*. No community is an island; what one does impacts others and vice versa. Therefore, developing good character within a community means being in relationship with others, receiving and responding, listening and learning, and considering what virtues and behaviors result in the thriving and flourishing of all.

Second is responsibility as *accountability* for one's moral failings. Developing character necessarily means becoming more aware of and confronting one's own failures. This means not allowing that to result in the paralysis of guilt, but recognizing our limitations, structural barriers, and the need to seek forgiveness and work in community with those who have been harmed by our privilege. To acknowledge our shortcomings and keep trying anyway, without being constrained by self-justification.

Third is responsibility as *responsiveness* to the most marginalized. This naturally flows from the recognition of one's privilege—as Bonhoeffer says, "bearing the burden of the other" and asking how Christ might take form today, on their behalf.[19] Responsibility is being responsible to and for others, responding to them in the context of their own situation, struggle, and concerns, prioritizing the self-determined needs of those with less privilege.

As I have confessed from the beginning, this book advocates for a virtue-oriented ethic that seeks liberation for all as its ultimate goal through the cultivation of communities of character. A communitarian virtue ethic of liberation draws on all three models to some degree while prioritizing the formation of character, for all the reasons above. I also contend that it actually embodies the most "realist" approach, especially for privileged Christians seeking to leverage our privilege and power in ways that shape our communities to be communities *for* others, especially the marginalized and oppressed. These efforts will often fall short, but a virtue ethic calls us all to keep trying, practicing, and working to develop the character necessary to bring about God's liberation for all.

Notes

1 "The Good Place," Season 3, Episode 10.
2 Karen Guth's work on moral failure is important in this context, and for thinking beyond it. She argues, "We need approaches that attend not only to the problems moral failure presents and concerns about human responsibility, but also to the potential goods of moral failure and to God's grace," ("The Potential Goods of Moral Failure," *Studies in Christian Ethics* 38 no.2 (2025): 86–104). Guth's work on the goods of moral failure follows similar and important work on tainted moral legacies. See *The Ethics of Tainted Legacies: Human Flourishing After Traumatic Pasts* (Cambridge, UK: Cambridge University Press, 2022).
3 For Niebuhr's thought on the atomic bomb, see Reinhold Niebuhr, "The Atomic Issue," *Christianity and Crisis* (October 15, 1945) among others.
4 Melanie Harris, *Gifts of Virtue, Alice Walker, and Womanist Ethics* (New York: Palgrave McMillan, 2010), 113, 114.
5 Derek Parfit, *On What Matters* (Oxford, UK: Oxford University Press, 2011).
6 James Cone, *God of the Oppressed* (New York: Orbis Books, 1975), 104.
7 Cone, *God of the Oppressed*, 105; *The Spirituals and the Blues* (Maryknoll, NY: Orbis Books, 1972), 100.
8 Dylan Mathews, "How *The Good Place* Taught Moral Philosophy to its Characters—and its Creators," *Vox* (January 30, 2020): http: https://www.vox.com/future-perfect/2019/9/26/20874217/the-good-place-series-finale-season-4-moral-philosophy.
9 Aristotle, *Rhetoric*, I:9, 1367a18-20; *Nicomachean Ethics*, 1130a4-9.
10 Katie G. Cannon, *Black Womanist Ethics* (Atlanta, GA: Scholars Press, 1988), 55.
11 Harris, 113, 114.
12 Harris, 87.
13 Harris, 66.
14 Lisa Tessman, *Burdened Virtues: Virtue Ethics for Liberatory Struggles* (Oxford, UK: Oxford University Press, 2005), 11, 16.
15 Tessman, 12, 13.
16 Tessman, 20.

17 Tessman, 76.
18 Harris, 122.
19 Dietrich Bonhoeffer, *Life Together and Prayerbook of the Bible*, *DBWE 5*, ed. Geoffrey B. Kelly, trans. James H. Burtness and Daniel W. Bloesch (Minneapolis, MN: Fortress Press, 2005), 101.

3

Worship and Justice

Introduction: Passing the Peace

A few years ago, I was doing research for a project that led me to First & Franklin Presbyterian Church in Baltimore. In a conversation with the worship pastor, he mentioned the way that the liturgical practice of the Passing of the Peace had been morally formative for this congregation. The Passing of the Peace had not always been a regular part of their worship. But the church initiated this practice back in 1986 in the midst of the HIV/AIDS crisis. First & Franklin had been the first church in the area willing to partner with a local HIV clinic in the early 1980s. This type of outreach to those neglected by most churches became a staple practice at First & Franklin, and the Passing of the Peace became a way to make this inclusive hospitality a regular and tangible part of the church's worship. One member told me, "We pass the peace in this church because Pastor Harry Hoefelder said in 1986, 'We are not going to be afraid to touch our neighbors.'" People were still afraid of the disease spreading through touch in the late 1980s, so people who were HIV positive essentially became "untouchables." Extending the Passing of the Peace to everyone who came through the doors gave them "at least once a week where they knew somebody was going to give them a hug." One member I spoke with recalled that "you would have people just come and sit in the back of the church and cry for an hour because they couldn't believe they found a church that would include them."

We tend to think about moral actions in terms of making choices. I still tell my child every morning on the way to school,

"Make good choices today." But in reality, ethics is not primarily about making right choices. As someone committed to a virtue ethics perspective, I would argue that it's about being shaped and formed into someone who does not make choices based on calculations of outcomes or precedent, but embodies ways of being and moving in the world because they have allowed God to shape them. This does not remove agency as a key component of the moral life, but suggests that one's agency is determined by the forces one has been shaped by, both voluntarily and involuntarily. While some social and moral conditioning happens to us in unconscious ways, we can also place ourselves in positions to be shaped by certain forces and contexts and invoke an awareness of what forces and contexts are forming us and how. And this is where the idea of practices and worship comes into focus.

The task of this chapter is to put together the pieces of a communitarian virtue ethics of liberation, beginning with the importance of cultivating habits through practices. The practice of Passing the Peace extended warmth and welcome to First & Franklin's neighbors, but it also shaped this congregation into one that welcomed all. It cultivated a congregational character that led it to seek more ways of doing justice in the community, leading it to become one of the most socially progressive churches in the city. This virtue of radical inclusion had become a habit cultivated through the liturgical practice of the Passing of the Peace. As a Christian virtue ethic, then, a discussion of virtue, habits, and practices ought to begin with worship.

Ethics and Worship Practices

One of the central forms of practice in the Christian faith is corporate worship. Now worship is primarily directed to God. It is the worship and adoration of, or our expression of love toward, God. As the opening lines of the Eucharist liturgy begin, "It is right and a good and joyful thing, always and everywhere to give our thanks to you." But worship also does something to the one worshiping. It is formative for the community doing it because worship follows a liturgy: a set of rituals and practices. And this is true whether you worship in a high church tradition or a low church tradition. Even rural Baptists and Pentecostals have a liturgy—a particular and consistent practice of worship, even if it is not printed in a lengthy bulletin or pages of the hymnal. Liturgy is a work conducted by human hands, minds, voices, and bodies. It may be primarily directed toward God, but, crucially, it also shapes the one doing the worshiping.

The worship practices a church engages in are not only spiritually formative but socially and ethically formative. As I mentioned in Chapter 1, the *Didache*, the original "Book of Common Prayer" for the early church, outlined liturgical practices as well as moral prescriptions for the church. It also intertwined worship and ethics seamlessly as if they were one and the same. It called them both a form of "training." The writer of the book of Hebrews understood the formative potential of Christian practices, writing of moral growth from milk to solid food "for those whose faculties have been trained by practice to distinguish good from evil" (5:14). In this way, worship and ethics have been bound together in the Christian life from its very beginning. Worship shapes us morally by providing a means to let the life of Jesus affect our morals and identity. The liturgy is like learning to perform a musical instrument, play a sport, or bake a cake. As you practice, it becomes second nature, and its repetition shapes your character. To put it in the faith of my upbringing—it draws you closer to the character of God.

Sunday Rituals and Everyday Ethics

A major proponent of a postliberal virtue approach to Christian ethics is Stanley Hauerwas. In fact, a major textbook organized and edited by Hauerwas and the Anglican priest Sam Wells structures its treatment of ethical issues and methodology around particular worship practices. They argue in one of the introductory chapters of that book, "The liturgy offers ethics a series of ordered practices that shape the character and assumptions of Christians, and suggest habits and models that inform every aspect of corporate life."[1] This text, as the introduction to a textbook, was meant to suggest the ways specific liturgical practices might shape us. While this book was extremely formative of my own view of ethics, and while today I don't agree with its entirety, they are not the only scholars and clergy reflecting on the connection between piety and politics, between worship and ethics.

Womanist ethicist Traci West likewise argues that "The rituals of Sunday worship enable Christians to publicly rehearse what it means to uphold the moral values they are supposed to bring to every aspect of their lives, from their attitudes about public policy to their intimate relations."[2] Worship is a rehearsal, a practicing of the habits that allow us to sustain our highest values. Ethics is about becoming a certain type of person, about the formation of character and identity. Worship practices, she says, may reinforce or they may challenge the cultural norms of society, and thus worship is crucial for a liberative ethic.

If, as James Cone argues, Christian theology must relate the confession of faith to the practice of political justice, then of course, worship must inevitably shape a social ethic—whether worship fosters just action or the maintenance of the status quo.[3] Any social ethic is fostered by concrete practices within the Christian community. As he notes, during the Civil Rights Movement, many political strategy sessions were conducted in the context of church worship. But beyond such direct political interventions, he argues that worship is bound to ethics because faith is bound to action.[4] He draws on Dietrich Bonhoeffer, who famously wrote that "Only those who are obedient can believe."[5] He contends, drawing on James's maxim that "faith without works is dead," that faith is only real when it leads to obedience and—going a step further—"faith only becomes faith in the act of obedience."[6]

Cone goes on to suggest that this linkage of faith and action is due to the intrinsic political nature of the Gospel. In modern, Western Christianity—especially the Evangelical model in which I grew up—faith is individualized and internalized. The Gospel was simply a means of obtaining eternal life in heaven. But this misses a significant social and public dimension of faith in the Gospel—noted by Cone, the writer of James, and others. In my conservative Baptist faith, we had no problem understanding that faith was fostered through practices like prayer, Bible reading, devotional "quiet time," and ascetic practices. We understood piety as constituted by practices that we engaged in to shape our loves, identities, and way of life. But this was purely personal and individual. And though our understanding stopped there, it only takes a step further to acknowledge that in this understanding of piety, rituals of worship are performed as a way of training and realizing piety in the entirety of a community's life.

This is an Aristotelian model of ethical pedagogy, in which external performative acts, like prayer, are understood to create corresponding inward dispositions, but on a communal level. Virtue is developed according to a correlation of outward behaviors, like prayer, and inward dispositions, like gratitude, and through repeated performance of acts that entail those particular virtues. Even the most ordinary church practices work in deep (and often unrecognized) ways to shape the hearts, minds, *and actions* of the people who attend these churches. Practices traditionally deemed merely spiritual can also be *political* because communal practices are formative of human dispositions and affections, as well as community identities, ones that often extend into public affairs and behaviors. Worship is an ethical act that both expresses social and political commitments and—reflectively—shapes our souls, minds, and bodies in ways that conform to or challenge our political and ethical commitments.

Practice, Habit, Character

I'll trace this argument following Augustine, who claimed that humans are motivated primarily by love. We are created by God with a desire to worship, a desire to love something, which means that we inhabit the world not fundamentally as thinkers, but as worshippers. In fact, *what* we love defines who we are; it *makes* us who we are. The object of our love will determine the type of person we become, the community we become part of, and the types of behaviors in which we will engage.[7] We begin to live in a way that expresses the nature of the object of our love. Our life will look different if our ultimate desire is to secure a high-paying financial sector job than if it is to care for endangered manatees.

Next, we cultivate this love for a particular object or vision of life through practices. This is where worship enters the picture. Worship practices are routines and rituals that train our hearts to desire or love certain things, shape our dispositions and character, and orient us toward a certain vision of life until they become woven into our character. The ordinary practices of congregations—from their method of communion to the songs they sing, to the way they make leadership decisions, or decide with whom to partner in ministry—form them in ways that suggest something about their ultimate love, as well as continue to shape and direct that love.[8]

Drawing on Augustine as I just have, Evangelical theologian James K. A. Smith follows this line, arguing that worship is not merely something humans do but what we are made for. Descartes's famous maxim—I think, therefore I am—is at best incomplete. It is love that forms our knowledge; humans are shaped from the *body up* rather than *head down*. That is, what we love is instilled in us through bodily practices.[9] To put this less theologically, cognitive scientists have found that environmental cues—like those that surround us and engage us during worship (kneeling, singing, eating, greeting one another with peace)—literally shape our brain development (and even do so in ways that can be passed down to future generations like living memories). What they call "linguistic signifiers," or these environmental cues or patterns of organizing bodies, speech, and habits, shape our patterns of thinking and social imaginations. In other words, embodied practices shape our social and moral imaginations in conscious and unconscious ways—for good and for bad.

Returning to worship, for example, Christians take the elements of a simple meal, bread and wine, and see new and subversive possibilities in them. For Christians, these ordinary elements are infused with meaning and memory of Christ's life and death. The meal attests to the unity of the congregational Body as it eats the Body of Christ and witnesses to the alternative economic ethics of the church, where all are welcome to feast regardless of social or economic status (1 Cor. 11:17-33). Through this meal, Christians affirm their commitment to Christ above all, reach out to those who are physically hungry, thirsty, or marginalized, and anticipate a future meal where everyone is welcome and everyone will have their fill.

Sam Wells, the Anglican ethicist who co-wrote the ethics textbook mentioned previously, reminds us that "Ethics is not about being clever in a crisis but about forming a character that does not realize it has been in a crisis until the crisis is over." Moral action becomes second nature. He outlines how that works within a virtue framework, as advocated in this book:

> Virtues are derived from repeated *practices* that a community continually performs because it regards them as central to its identity. Repeated *practice* nurtures *skill*, an excellence that derives from repeated performance. *Skill* develops *habit*, a disposition to use skills on occasions and in locations different from the times and places where the skill was developed. *Habit* develops *instinct*, a pattern of unconscious behavior that reveals a deep element of *character*.[10]

James Clear, in a popular self-help book on developing good habits, makes an important point about character development. The process of formation must begin by focusing not on what you want to achieve but on who you want to become. He offers an example: "Imagine two people resisting a cigarette." When Person 1 is offered one, they respond, "No thanks. I'm trying to quit." While this sounds like a reasonable response, he notes that this person "still believes they are a smoker who is trying to be something else." When Person 2 is offered a smoke, they respond, "No thanks. I'm not a smoker." This is a subtle change in response, but it signals a change in identity, a process of formation directed not toward an outcome but an identity that makes a certain outcome sustainable. "Habits are how you embody your identity," he concludes, and also how you achieve it.[11]

Virtue ethics is about developing habits, not for their own sake, but as a process of formation—becoming the type of person or community who lives out the Gospel. Clear notes, "A habit is a behavior that has been repeated enough times to become automatic."[12] When a person first encounters a new situation, or a new moral problem, they have to decide, "How do I respond to this?" But once moral habits are created by repeated practice, the person no longer must analyze the situation or calculate the outcome—they respond automatically because they have developed an identity of good character. The response is now part of their character.

This means Christians must reflect on the ways practices, including liturgical practices and everyday quotidian habits, shape our identities and vision of the good life. For example, might the practice of confession engender in us a humility that informs our public and political posture toward those with whom we disagree, might taking the Eucharist instill in us an eagerness to feed those who are literally starving, or might our veneration of the cross evoke the bodies of African Americans lynched by mobs of white Christians, as James Cone suggests, and compel us to resist racial injustice?

Deformative Liturgies, or Christians Behaving Badly

But also, what if they don't? That is, what happens when practices like the Eucharist or confession do not turn us into better people, a community closer to the heart of God? What is it that leads the Apostle Paul to confess: "I do not do the good I want to do, but the evil I do not want to do—this I keep on doing" (Rom. 7:19)? It seems this is too often the case, actually. This book began with the history of the slave trade, which involved sanctuaries of worshipers sitting directly atop slave dungeons, after all. Additionally, if this account of formative practices is true, then practices can shape our moral imaginations in sinister ways as well. For example, recall my reference to linguistic signifiers. Much research has been done on how these environmental cues, like seeing gated communities or imbibing racial stereotypes on television, shape our racial imaginations in harmful, racist ways. Even these involuntary practices that may make up the "background" of our lives have formative and malformative potential to shape our morality.

And so, the concern becomes that theologians so focused on Christian practices often project abstract or ideal accounts of worship practices and their effects. For example, James K.A. Smith claims that the reason Christian worship does not always create a people who look like Christ—the reason that some Christians attend worship regularly and still behave badly—is due to the worldly, cultural liturgies that compete with the church for control of our hearts.[13] The problem, in this reasoning, is that Christians can be conscripted by these rival kingdoms or the church assimilates to *worldly* politics, identities, and practices—when worldly liturgies occasionally win out in this competition for our hearts. White supremacy, for example, is the result of a rival tradition, of worldly influences, forming us; it is not inherent to the church's tradition itself. In these accounts, however, the misperformance of Christian practice, or the damage that ensues from practice, is left out of the picture. And when vice is taken into account, blame is placed on forces external to the church and its practice of these idealized rituals.

But this cannot always be true. For example, slavery was not predicated on a "worldly" imagination, but on a scriptural imagination that invoked passages about slaves remaining obedient to masters. White supremacy is not a result of the church assimilating to the world or being coopted by worldly liturgies. Rather, as I noted in the introduction, it is a result in part of liturgies and practices inherent to the church itself—malforming liturgies and practices that the church actually gave to the world. Theologian Willie Jennings indicts Christianity in the development of white supremacy through its collusion with what he calls a "diseased social imagination" of colonialism and European superiority.[14] Recall that Kelly Brown Douglas suggested that if Christianity has been used for so much oppression, there must be something wrong with Christianity itself.[15]

Consequently, white supremacy is the product of what we might call Christianity's *diseased theological imagination*. The church established the framework through which Europeans would make sense of the differently-bodied others they encountered through colonial exploration and conquest.[16] White identity was taking shape as a theological identity born out of European attempts to make sense of their encounter with people who did not fit into their pre-established Christian account of insiders and pagans.[17] Whiteness indicated a high probability of salvation and then moved along a sliding scale of darkness, with Black bodies being the least likely to be saved—except perhaps through force or slavery. Whiteness had become the marker of true Christianity: God's chosen people. All others—those in need of conversion, often through the catechetical method of slavery—were organized around this racial center. "The Christian theological imagination was woven into a process of colonial dominance," Jennings writes. "Other peoples and their ways of life had to adapt, become fluid, even morph into the colonial order of things."[18] As Douglas puts it, Christianity provided a "sacred canopy" for racism, and thus found its own tradition malformed and continually malforming in the wake of this alliance.[19] Attributing it to the world outside the church obscures the role of Christianity in its development as well as our responsibility to contest it.

"Many current discussions of Christian practice are too rosy—are pristinated," argues Anglican theologian Lauren Winner, "and fail to acknowledge, let alone account for or respond to, the sin entailed *by* those practices."[20] Of course, some things do go wrong in uncharacteristic ways. That is, they are damaged or deformed externally, from the outside. But some go wrong in characteristic ways, deformations intimate with the form and goods of the liturgical practice itself.

Winner takes concrete cases and displays, for example, the ways the internal logic of the Eucharist—consuming the Jewish flesh of Christ—generated the deformed medieval "host desecration narratives" that falsely accused Jews of attempting to destroy the Eucharistic wafer and often led to their execution. As European Christians came to venerate the host, their reverence for the practice buttressed their Christian identity in ways that heightened their sense of religious superiority and further "othered" the Jews whom they encountered every day. Their reverence for one heightened their hatred for the other. She says that a practice in which Christians consumed the Jewish flesh of Christ resulted in Christians destroying the literal Jewish flesh of their neighbors.

Scholars like Orlando Patterson and Saidiya Hartman offer stories of Africans captured by European colonizers and traffickers, taken to dungeons on the coast and literally baptized into a destiny of slavery.[21] Or for a more contemporary example, Traci West claims that intercessory prayers for the less fortunate and vulnerable "others," as well as prayers of thanksgiving for how God has blessed "us," might undergird a sense of entitlement to material "blessings." And, when performed within a predominantly white setting, it might even confuse "blessing" with entitlement to material white privilege.[22]

Practices like the Eucharist, baptism, or prayer carry within themselves the possibilities of their own deformation. They can be used in logically consistent ways for evil ends, and they can shape us in evil ways. For many, the historic complicity of these practices may suggest that the church cannot reform itself from within, relying on the morally formative powers of its practices. These somewhat nihilistic perspectives have, reasonably, determined that the church is inescapably lost. Images of burning crosses, Nazi flags hanging above altars, or, more recently, of those carrying crosses to the Capitol insurrection on January 6 provide strong evidence in favor of this belief.

Liberative Liturgy

Yet, others believe in the ethically transformative power of worship, though this can only be accomplished with a sober recognition of the ways these liturgical practices have been deployed toward injustice and violence. This also requires a historical awareness of the way in which they have the internal potential for deformation. Catholic womanist theologian M. Shawn Copeland recognizes that since racism and other forms of domination and oppression infiltrate and corrupt "the institutions of politics, economy, culture, even religion" and even our own bodies, purely cognitive modes of resistance will remain inadequate. In *Enfleshing Freedom*, she argues that corrupt practices must be challenged by *embodied* practices of solidarity— even within worship. She identifies Eucharist and table fellowship as practices that may challenge racist ideologies because of their power and political implications.

Though the Eucharist has been a trigger of supersessionist and racist violence, according to Copeland and evidenced above by Winner, the radical bodily inclusion that is also inherent to the practice makes it a possible means of liberation for the oppressed and a mode of repentance and solidarity on the part of the privileged. This is due to the ways it appreciates bodily differences while still bonding bodies together in the consuming of "one body." Bodies of different colors, nationalities, abilities, and political beliefs all eat from bread designated as the one Body of Christ. Perhaps this is as simple as reminding congregants of the biblical injunction to "go first and be reconciled" to one another before partaking in the Eucharist (Mt. 5:24). How would that change a congregation's approach to Communion? It can also function as a "countersign" to the devaluing of Black bodies by serving as a memorial for all of those who, like Jesus, are victims of oppression. In the "humble embrace of different bodies," Copeland claims, "Eucharistic celebration forms our social imagination, transvalues our values, and transforms the meaning of our being human, of embodying Christ." In other words, it cultivates character.

Traci West also points to Communion as a liturgical means of liberation, but she insists that Communion must be reimagined and church leadership must be explicit about making these connections. She gives an example of just this type of reimagining of worship: "As a way of commemorating the execution of Jesus by the Roman state, his suffering that preceded it, and the resurrection that followed it, the Communion ritual could highlight a range of cultural contexts where the suffering due to state-sponsored terrorism and killing has occurred in the past or present." In order to make this argument a little more concrete, let me point to a few examples of churches attempting to consciously think about the ways worship practices might transform their practice of ethics.

Baptism and Black Lives Matter

In the summer of 2020, during the Black Lives Matter protests that followed the murder of George Floyd, African American religion scholar and pastor Brad Braxton suggested including a "roll call" of martyred names during baptism services, including those killed in the struggle for Black freedom. "When Jesus stepped into the Jordan River to be baptized, he signed his death certificate," Braxton claims. Baptism represents "a marking of our bodies for struggle." Braxton now precedes baptisms with the names of Addie Mae Collins, Cynthia Wesley, Carole Robertson, and Carol Denise McNair, the four girls killed in the bombing of the 16th Street Baptist Church in Birmingham in 1963. But he also voices the names of George Floyd, Breonna Taylor, and Ahmaud Arbery as those who were baptized into the struggle because they were executed by state-sanctioned violence. Braxton says it is important to call attention to the political implications of ordinary church practices like this in order to make it apparent to baptismal candidates that this liturgical practice calls them to a costly discipleship.[23]

Preaching and Ebenezer Baptist

A few years ago, I lived in Atlanta and attended Ebenezer Baptist Church, whose former pastors included Martin Luther King Sr. and

Jr., and was now pastored by Raphael Warnock. I also remember a Sunday morning just before the 2008 election and years before Warnock would become a US Senator, when he preached from Num. 13:25-31, the story of the Hebrew spies returning from their venture into Canaan with dire news of the overwhelming size of its inhabitants. He likened this narrative to the story of African American struggles, claiming that when no other spy trusted God or thought victory was possible, Caleb exclaimed, "Yes we can!"— an overt reference to Barack Obama's campaign slogan. The church then had voter registration tables set up in the narthex following the service. Beyond mere partisan promotion, this was one instance in a consistent pattern in worship at Ebenezer of lifting up the community, promoting dignity, achievement, and pride within the Black community, as well as a reminder of the inherently political nature of the Gospel.

Confession and Mount Vernon Place

On October 8, 2017, on the 100th anniversary of the laying of the sanctuary cornerstone, Mount Vernon Place United Methodist Church in downtown Washington, DC, offered a service of Remembrance and Repentance for its role in slavery. In her sermon that day, Pastor Donna Claycomb Sokol explained how conversations during a congregational book series on racial justice sparked a desire to learn more about the history of the congregation and what the words "Methodist Episcopal Church South," engraved into the white marble façade of the sanctuary, actually meant: a denomination that splintered off in 1844 to uphold the right of its members to own slaves. Mount Vernon Place was soon founded in 1850 to be the "representative" church of the Methodist Episcopal Church South, and its slaveholding values, in the heart of the nation's capital. As she ended the sermon, she explained, "We cannot change what people most treasured in the past. But we can repent.... We can turn away from whatever has a grip on us, and reorient our lives to a vision of God's best ways for the world."

To conclude the service, the church engaged in a "Confessional Litany of Remembrance and Repentance" to "name the sin of racism and repent for our roots in white supremacy." They concluded by asking for forgiveness, not just for themselves, but also for "those who came before us." After this service, the words "We repent for our roots in white supremacy" were printed on a large banner that the congregation signed and hung from the columns of the church building. This act of public confession unto repentance is certainly not sufficient, as Sokol would say, but represents one way in which congregations can publicly practice virtue. Such practices hold the power and potential for liberation. However, the social and political implications of worship must be made explicit, while their potential for malformation must be raised as well.

In worship we train ourselves to discover "who Christ is for us today," and how we might embody Christ's presence in a world searching for answers. This means that, in the end, when we worship in our congregations, we are not only worshiping God but we are allowing God to form us into God's people in the world:

When we greet one another with the Peace of Christ, we commit to working for physical peace for the world and for our enemies, and welcome one another into God's family despite differences in appearance, political persuasions, sexual orientation, race, or gender identity.

When we confess our sins, we open ourselves humbly to the sinful realities of the world and the deepest struggles of humanity, recognize the ways that we are embedded in systems that thrive on other people's oppression, and commit to working for reparative just action.

When we perform a baptism, we are witnessing to the fact that our penultimate identities of nation, sex, race, and class are all overcome by our new identity and allegiance to Christ, and commit to overcoming all social divisions that create inequity.

When we break bread in the Eucharist, we remember those who do not have daily bread and commit to working for a day when everyone can give thanks for the abundance God offers and the overcoming of injustices that make it so that some go without.

A Communitarian Virtue Ethic of Liberation

Finally, we have arrived at the conclusion of Part I, a hopefully not-too-dry overview of the context and methods for Christian ethics. This account of worship practices is where the commitments to liberation and virtue ethics intersect. These two theological and ethical traditions have often been contrasted, pitted against one another as either a stabilizing force for the status quo or revolutionary and radical, pushing the boundaries of Christian theology. But as their shared commitments to community, context, and formation suggest, they are not mutually exclusive. In some ways, we might see liberation as the end and virtue as the process—shaping communities to follow a liberated Jesus into the margins to struggle alongside the oppressed.

These traditions also align with much of feminist and womanist thought—while also benefiting from their insights. What these perspectives contribute to the methodology of virtue ethics is to press the question of formative influences wider than typical virtue ethics or postliberal approaches do. To this discussion, we might also add the practices of other, overlapping communities that might inform Christian behavior and provide us with other formative practices directed toward liberation. Like Jesus learning from the Syrophoenician woman, womanist and feminist theology affirm the communal location of postliberal virtue ethics, but add that liberation cannot be achieved unless the church community learns from those that it has historically pushed to the margins. Its witness must be shaped by witnessing their concerns, perspectives, and insights. These commitments together help produce the communitarian virtue ethic of liberation that animates these pages.

Before moving on to Part II and addressing the way someone shaped by this communitarian virtue ethic of liberation might consider urgent moral issues of today, let me summarize a few crucial elements of this approach, which are also shared resources from postliberal, liberationist, feminist, and womanist thought, in broad strokes.

Context

First, these ethical emphases are grounded in a core commitment to contextuality. With all due respect to the Beatles, there is no "man from nowhere" with "no point of view" from which a person can objectively observe and choose between differing truths or moral claims. As finite creatures and moral agents, we are unable to see the world clearly or in whole; again, we see partly, through a glass dimly, restricted by the contingencies of our subjective experience. The very idea that someone could occupy a neutral view from nowhere is already a view from a particular location—that of privilege, of never having to question your own position as normative—and has been shaped by a particular social context. All perspectives begin from a particular standpoint or context that has been shaped by a person or community's history, relationships, experience, knowledge, and limitations. And all ethical reasoning and judgments derive from that context and are in many ways bound to it. What is virtuous in some contexts may not be in others.

Community

This means that our moral lives are developed in community. I like to consider myself a nonconformist, but even as I try to resist the opinions of those around me, I am still thinking through issues and decisions as part of a community. American individualism teaches us to pull ourselves up by our bootstraps, but even those bootstraps were made by someone else, and my ability to pull myself up will impact someone else around me in ways I may never consider. I may have been shaped by multiple communities, like a Venn diagram (a Baptist, academic, from the South, with commitments to a particular family and to friends), but my thinking and moral agency are still conditioned by and bound to those communities. That is, I'm not only shaped by a community or communities, but also morally connected to them and responsible to them: what I do impacts those communities and vice versa. Relationality is inevitable and at times can lead to harm (I may perpetuate the damage and trauma inflicted on me by a community onto that same community or onto others) or to good (I learn from multiple communities and can help shape others to be more caring and compassionate).

Character

This way of thinking about how we learn and develop as moral agents leads to an ethical methodology directed toward character development. That is, recognizing the limits of our contextuality as well as the importance of community means that a) our ability to determine what action will lead to the best ethical outcome or consequence for the most people is hubris and b) the moral duties or rules we choose to guide our decision-making will not be the same as those others choose as they are shaped by and bound to other communities and contexts. Instead, we must live into our contextuality and commonality, and strive to develop the character required to live morally within and across communities of difference.

Virtue is often considered an individualized ethic (and has often functioned this way in its original Aristotelian sense). But this sense of virtue neglects the communal nature of moral agency mentioned above. We do not develop character in a vacuum nor for self-justification. Our relationality and the contextual limits of our own knowledge prohibit that. Rather, we develop character through a process of relationality and mutuality, as a community of responsibility for and to others. As followers of Jesus, interpreting Jesus with the tools available to us, this at least means developing virtues of compassion, openness, and care as we recognize our limits as well as the harms we have inflicted and injustices in which we are enmeshed.

Formation

An ethic of character development, then, necessarily proceeds in formation. We are inevitably formed by the environments and practices that make up our daily lives, but we must choose to live into practices that form us into disciples of Jesus. As mentioned previously, this means we practice with a sober realization of the ways Christian practices have produced harm and injustice. This necessitates an open rather than closed formation. The guides that form us are certainly within our community of faith, but also those outside of our community and context—those who provide a different perspective and critical eye, especially those whose voices have historically been marginalized and even silenced. Like Jesus and the Canaanite woman, or congregations listening to the voices of LGBTQ people who are hurt by the church, or denominations listening to Black Lives Matter activists, these are the clouds of witnesses calling us to bear their witness, learn from it, and allow it to alter our practices, habits, and character. Moral formation is a humble process of vulnerability and openness to change.

Justice

Finally, formation is always directed toward an end. As Miroslav Volf and his co-teachers explain to students in their popular "Life Worth Living" course, "We need practices to pursue a way of life for the long-haul. Those practices have to correspond to the vision of life we are trying to pursue."[24] A communitarian virtue ethic of liberation must still be directed toward an end or a way of life—a life dedicated to justice and the liberation of all people. For privileged Christians wondering what following Jesus means in this world of ethical ambiguity, it starts with allowing ourselves to be led by those on the margins: allowing those communities to infiltrate our communities of privilege, to challenge our contexts and open new vistas of perception, to shape our formative practices, and to guide us toward liberative action. It is only in the liberation of those the privileged Christian church has historically oppressed and continues to harm that we can liberate ourselves from these same systems.

In Part II, I will take this communitarian virtue ethic of liberation, as incomplete and imperfect as it is, and consider how one shaped by these crucial elements might approach six of the most urgent moral issues today. For most of these, the church has found itself on the wrong side of history—or in most cases, shaping that history in unjust ways. I want us to consider how this ethical model might help us to reimagine how we frame, deliberate, and act on these issues.

Notes

1 Stanley Hauerwas and Samuel Wells, "Christian Ethics as Informed Prayer," in *Blackwell Companion to Christian Ethics*, ed. Hauerwas and Wells (Oxford, UK: Blackwell, 2004), 7.

2 Traci West, *Disruptive Christian Ethics: When Racism and Women's Lives Matter* (Louisville, KY: Westminster John Knox Press, 2006), 112.

3 James H. Cone, "Christian Faith and Political Praxis," *Encounter* 43, no. 2 (1982): 129–41, 138.

4 Cone, 131, 136.

5 Dietrich Bonhoeffer, *Discipleship, Dietrich Bonhoeffer Works (English)*, vol. 4, ed. John Godsey and Geffrey B. Kelly, trans. Reinhard Krauss and Barbara Green (Minneapolis, MN: Fortress Press, 2003), 63.

6 Cone, 138.

7 "If we are to discover the character of any people, we have only to examine what it loves," Augustine, *City of God*, ed. R.W. Dyson (Cambridge, UK: Cambridge University Press, 1998), 19.24.

8 For an analytical history of this shift toward attending to practices as formative and constitutive of identity, see Manuel A. Vasquez, *More Than Belief: A Materialist Theory of Religion* (Oxford, UK: Oxford University Press, 2010), 211–60.

9 James K. A. Smith, *Desiring the Kingdom: Worship, Worldview, and Cultural Formation* (Ada, MI: Baker Academic, 2009), 58, 80.

10 Samuel Wells, *Improvisation: The Drama of Christian Ethics* (Ada, MI: Brazos Press, 2004), 24 (emphasis mine).

11 James Clear, *Atomic Habits: An Easy and Proven Way to Build Good Habits and Break Bad Ones* (New Hyde Park, NY: Avery Publishing, 2018), 32.

12 Clear, 22, 44.

13 James K. A. Smith, *Awaiting the King: Reforming Public Theology* (Grand Rapids, MI: Baker Publishing, 2017), 168.

14 Willie Jennings, *The Christian Imagination* (New Haven: Yale University Press, 2011), 6, 9.

15 Kelly Brown Douglas, *What's Faith Got to Do with It? Black Bodies/Christian Souls* (Maryknoll, NY: Orbis Books, 2005), xiii.

16 Jennings, 26.

17 James W. Perkinson, *White Theology: Outing Supremacy in Modernity* (New York: Palgrave Macmillan, 2004), 155.

18 Jennings, 8.

19 Douglas, 9.

20 Lauren Winner, *The Dangers of Christian Practice: On Wayward Gifts, Characteristic Damage, and Sin* (New Haven, CT: Yale University Press, 2018), 167.

21 Orlando Patterson, *Slavery and Social Death: A Comparative Study*, 1st ed. (Cambridge, MA: Harvard University Press, 1985); Saidiya Hartman, *Lose Your Mother: A Journey Along the Atlantic Slave Route* (New York: Farrar, Straus & Giroux, 2008).

22 West, 119.

23 Braxton, "Baptism and Holy Communion: Affirming that Black Lives Matter," in *T&T Clark Handbook of African American Theology*, ed. Antonia Michelle Daymond, Frederick L. Ware, and Eric Lewis Williams (Edinburgh: T&T Clark, 2020), 197–221.

24 See Miroslav Volf, Matthew Croasmun, and Ryan McAnnally-Linz, *Life Worth Living: A Guide to What Matters Most* (New York: The Open Field, 2023).

PART II

Christian Ethics in the World

4

Politics

Introduction: Changing the System

Recently, I was sitting in the basement hall of a local Black church, meeting with other community leaders and local organizers as we attempted to launch an Industrial Areas Foundation (IAF) chapter in my hometown. IAF is the leading broad-based, interfaith, multiracial community organizing network in the United States, with chapters in over sixty cities across the country and a proven track record of accomplishments—from affordable housing to educational equity to better healthcare access—all on the local level. It leverages the power of people and the institutions to which they belong—congregations, faith communities, nonprofits, neighborhood associations—to identify needed yet winnable issues, make specific practical proposals, and hold community and elected leaders accountable to their promises. I was new to the effort and to the area but had quickly caught up on the history of local political organizing. Over a year into the effort, several pastors of Black congregations raised the concern that their voices and issues were still being marginalized. A previous organizing effort was attempted years ago that eventually fragmented when issues that were deemed by some to be racial and radical arose as major concerns from the Black community. The white churches dropped out, creating years of division and distrust that linger and haunt this new effort. And sitting in that room, my mind drifted to a historical figure that had become important and personal to me.

A few years prior, I had begun a modest research project on Black freedom organizer Ella Baker. Baker would work for the NAACP and serve as director of Martin Luther King's Southern Christian Leadership Conference (SCLC) during the early civil rights movement. While charismatic leaders like King were mobilizing the masses, Baker was organizing them into effective action groups on the ground, in sit-ins, boycotts, and through leadership development that would sustain local movements even after the national leadership and spotlight moved on to other campaigns and cities.

As I sat in this church basement and peered at my Styrofoam cup of coffee, listening to the concerns of these Black clergy, I thought about a moment of crossroads in Baker's journey. Having grown disillusioned with the top-down approach and hero worship of much of the civil rights leadership, especially the male clergy leaders like King, Baker invited the student leaders of the new sit-in movement to a conference at Shaw University in Raleigh, NC, in early 1960. She was still wary of experienced leaders' tendency to move in and take control of local struggles because they felt that they were more capable. So, though she tended to participate primarily through active listening and guided direction, behind the scenes she protected students' autonomy in charting their own path. She wanted the student movement to remain unco-opted by a larger organization like the SCLC but to create their own. "My theory is, strong people don't need strong leaders," she would say. "In organizing a community, you start with people where they are."[1] Despite her quiet demeanor, she insisted on recognition on the part of the established powers that people have a right to participate in the decisions that affect their lives. That conference birthed the Student Nonviolent Coordinating Committee (SNCC), the most important community organizing effort in the movement. As her biographer Barbara Ransby comments, SNCC represented a shift from high-profile events to everyday grassroots organizing in local communities. SCLC was inspiration and mobilization; SNCC was organizing and sustainability.[2]

On a personal level for me, Baker grew up in my home state of North Carolina, her childhood home about two miles from my own grandmother's. Yet, in all my visits to the rural, farming town of Littleton, I never heard of her, likely because of her status as a Black woman in the movement and one who did not seek the spotlight. Her rearing in the Black Baptist Church—her grandfather was a pastor and perhaps the biggest influence on her life—and especially the women's missionary movement of which her mother was a member along with the collective farming community in Warren County served as a foundation for her "grassroots, group-centered leadership style, her egalitarian vision for a renewed society, and . . . [her belief that] as an African American woman, she had both the capacity and the obligation to be a powerful force for social change."[3] Her early church formation engendered a commitment to solidarity; shared resources and mutual obligation were what bound the rural Black church in which she grew up. And though her particular faith commitments would change and wane over the years, it was the politics of the rural Baptist church that shaped her political imagination to "[face] a system that does not lend itself to your needs and devising means by which you change that system."[4]

As in the lives and work of many civil rights leaders, their faith called them to political activism, to challenge the political forces that seek power over the vulnerable and marginalized. For a communitarian virtue ethics of liberation, the link between faith and politics is crucial. To effect any sort of liberation in the world requires engagement with political powers; yet this means that the Christian community must also stay awake to the ways the political powers shape our hearts, minds, and actions as well. To put it in contemporary terms, the relationship between faith and politics is complicated.

A Political Gospel

The complex relationship between Christian faith and politics is apparent in the very structure of American culture and government. The nineteenth-century French sociologist Alexis de Tocqueville made a perplexing observation during his time studying the United States in the 1830s. He said that while the United States operates with a formal separation of church and state, religion is the first of America's political institutions. Part of his discovery is that the political nature of the church in America exists in its *mores*—that is, the way it shapes the values and commitments of its members. It's not in explicit political statements, but in the way theological values seep into political actions.[5] This conclusion is echoed by womanist theologian Emilie Townes, who states that our political judgments inevitably contain implicit theological values, adding a word of caution that this means we must be self-aware of the ways our religious values shape our policy decisions.[6] A major study a few years back by scholars Robert Putnam and David Campbell discovered that nearly two hundred years after Tocqueville, the political significance of congregations still resides in their social networks. Political discussions happen not frequently from the pulpit but informally in small groups, Bible studies, and the church parlor. And what this leads to, they reveal, is a political like-mindedness, an echo chamber effect, generating the political congruence of people in a congregation—it's a self-reinforcing process. Most Christians attend a church of people who agree with them politically on nearly every single issue—and I think we've seen the consequences of that over the last couple of decades.[7]

So, this leads to the next question of how, in what ways, Christians ought to engage and interact in our public, social, and political contexts. What do we do in an American context in which church and state were established with a wall of separation between them? There is to be no favored or established religion in the state, and the state is not supposed to infringe on internal religious affairs. So, does this limit what we as people of faith can and should do in public?

According to liberation theologians like Gustavo Gutiérrez and James Cone, the Gospel is inherently political. Gutiérrez explains: "Jesus died at the hands of the political authorities, the oppressors of the Jewish people. According to Roman custom, the title on the cross indicated the reason for the sentence; in the case of Jesus, this title denoted political guilt: King of the Jews."[8] In fact, Jesus' ministry began with a political claim. When he returned to his hometown of Nazareth to officially begin his ministry, he first went to the synagogue. He stood up and read a mixture of selections from Isaiah: "The Spirit of the Lord is upon me, because he has anointed me to bring good news to the poor. He has sent me to proclaim release to the captives and recovery of sight to the blind, to let the oppressed go free, to proclaim the year of the Lord's favor" (Lk. 4:16-19).

From beginning to end, Jesus' ministry was about inaugurating an alternative form of politics in the world. As Evangelical scholar N. T. Wright puts it, "Jesus' launch of the kingdom—God's worldwide sovereignty on earth as it is in heaven—is the central aim of his mission, the thing for which he lived and died and rose again."⁹ But this was a different sort of political ruler, one who rules because he humbled himself unto death (Phil. 2:5-11); who sits on his throne in the form of a Lamb that was sacrificed (Rev. 5:6-7); who is proclaimed King while dying for the sake of the world (Mk 15:26). And this is a different sort of political reality, one that belongs to the little children, to tax collectors, and the destitute (Mk 10:14; Mt. 18:3; Mt. 21:31; Lk. 18:16); it is not run by the rich and powerful (Mt. 19:23; Mk 10:23; Lk. 18:24-25), but belongs to the poor (Lk. 6:20); it requires sacrifice and commitment, but also the posture of a servant: "the rulers in this world lord it over them . . . but not so with you" (Mt. 20:25-26).

In this light, when he announces what his ministry is about, Jesus offers a public statement, a public mission, a political theology—from the very beginning. It is not the case that theology became political or can be applied to politics, but the Gospel is political from the first proclamations of Christ. It is clear that following Jesus has to do with addressing social issues—poverty, health care, the prison system, systemic racism, and economic justice. As the theologians who have helped shape this book, like James Cone, Gustavo Gutiérrez, Emilie Townes, Kelly Brown Douglas, and Dietrich Bonhoeffer all claim, theology that attends to what Jesus was about must, therefore, be a political theology.

This means that the church must be politically engaged if it is to be faithful and if it is to work on behalf of the marginalized. In fact, the church's very beginning at Pentecost was a politically charged event (Acts 2:1-13). As Willie Jennings argues, by speaking the language of people of other nationalities, ethnicities, and political identities at its very first gathering, the church became a body that transgressed traditional political lines. The church's foundation required reconciliation between two ethnic, cultural, and social groups: Jew and Gentile (Eph. 2:14). From the beginning, the people of God have existed as a social and political reality. The church began, he writes, by "[upsetting] the particular ideological arrangements of nations, peoples, and corporations" at Pentecost. It launched a "new network of kinship that transgresses life-threatening and life-diminishing boundaries," and is called to continue this work.¹⁰ And therefore, at its foundation, the church itself is a political body. It is not withdrawn from the world, concerned only with spiritual things, with caring for souls. But if it is to remain true to following

Jesus' mission, then even its commitments to personal piety are acts that witness to this new political reality and direct our allegiance away from earthly powers to the one "ruler of the kingdoms of the earth" (Rev. 1:5). Faith is always personal, but never private. And in this sense, our faith itself is politics.

But Christianity's public, social, and political mission is also complicated. In the Gospels, we see Jesus tell his followers to pay taxes to a government that is busy using those funds to militarily tighten their own oppression (Mark 12). We see Paul commission Christians to submit to these same ruling authorities and tell us that all political authority is instituted by God and given certain powers of judgment (Romans 13). And we see John's prophetic vision in Revelation of an evil, corrupt political authority; one that blasphemously desires our worship and allegiance. And one that is ultimately struck down and overcome by a lamb that was slain (Revelation 13). So, what are we to make of these complex origin stories? How are Christians to act in public? How are we to relate to or engage in politics?

A Very Brief History of Christian Politics

Theologians have wrestled with the questions above for centuries and within a diverse set of social and political contexts. In many ways, you could say that the scholarly discipline of political theology began with Augustine—though, as I have said, politics was integral to the theology and practice of the church from its origin: from the writing of the Gospels, the *Didache*, the letters of Paul, and early writings of Tertullian, Justin Martyr, and others. Still, one of the earliest and most famous codified theological assessments of politics comes from Augustine. Writing during the collapse of the Roman Empire, Augustine begins anthropologically, observing—as we encountered in Chapter 3—that humans are creatures made to love and worship. Therefore, he defines politics as "an assembled multitude of rational creatures bound together by a common agreement as to the objects of their love. In this case, if we are to discover the character of any people, we have only to examine what it loves."[11] This means that what a community *is* can be discovered by what it worships. Political communities have a theological end, just like theological communities have a political end.

Because of this, says Augustine, Christians are to follow the customs and laws of earthly communities as long as they "do not impede the religion by which we are taught that the one supreme and true God is to be worshipped." Christians can make use of earthly goods and engage in earthly deliberations, in public, political, and social activities. We ought to make use of earthly goods and seek the peace of the earthly city, but we are not to be *captivated* by earthly goods—never to fall in love with them or worship any political leader, party, or platform.

Martin Luther, also writing during a time of political and religious upheaval in Europe, draws on his Augustinian roots to argue famously for his Two Kingdoms theology: this is the Kingdom of God (including the frighteningly small number of true believers under Christ) and the Kingdom of the World (earthly temporal political rule, or the use of the sword, for punishment of the wicked and protection of the righteous). He says that true Christians do not need the temporal law or sword when they are engaged with one another; they are guided by a higher spiritual ethic and do not use it among themselves. They follow the Gospel and the social life outlined in the Sermon on the Mount. But they cannot do this in their public duty. There they submit willingly as a service to their neighbor and willingly take up the sword in defense of the public good. "If anyone attempted to rule the world by the gospel," Luther writes, "he would be loosing the ropes and chains of the savage wild beasts and letting them bite and mangle everyone."[12] The most striking part of this theology is the way that it works to divide the individual Christian into a subject of two authorities—two kingdoms existing within one person, so to speak. Within this split identity, the *inner man*, as he calls it, is the person of faith, justified by grace through faith and in no need of good works to reconcile her to God.[13] She is obedient to God through faith, though her *outer man* must be obedient to external political authorities. God established governmental authority, so it would only make sense for Christians to take part in any service of God, including government. In fact, Luther goes a step further and insists that because Christians are to do what is beneficial for the world, they are under obligation to bear the sword in the kingdom of this world by whatever means they can: they should even be the first to volunteer as a hangman.[14]

Similarly, John Calvin also promoted a theology of two governments presiding over people. The duty of the earthly government is to protect the worship of God. In fact, Calvin goes a bit further than Luther in promoting religious establishment: the idea of a Christian state. Still, the government's exercise of force is compatible with Christian piety—because it is based on the authority of God—and Christians owe full obedience to the earthly ruler, even a corrupt and despotic ruler. Calvin does not leave much room for dissent or political disobedience, with one exception: if the laws and commands of the ruler lead the Christians away from obedience to God.[15]

Now these three have done much to shape the political imaginations and actions of Christians throughout history, and it's impossible not to see their imprint today. But again, we live in a different time and context, and a lot of political theology from a diverse set of voices works to reshape our vision of Christian political engagement. In fact, we must listen to these voices more urgently than ever as we begin to unravel the ways traditional political theology has inevitably led to two dangerous outcomes: political quietism and Christian nationalism. Political quietism is the belief that faith has nothing to do with politics but is an individualistic and interior matter. Christians, and especially church bodies, should not involve themselves in politics and should attempt to keep that wall of separation sturdy. This is a version of Luther's Two Kingdoms theology that attempts to keep faith uncorrupted from the ugly business of politics. I have written about this elsewhere and identified the way it trades in a shallow, even heretical theology. Wanting to keep these chapters accessibly brief, I'll allow my argument in that book to stand.[16] But this comes at a time when such prescriptions are more fraught than ever.

I write this chapter just a few weeks removed from Donald Trump's second electoral victory. I may not know the state of our politics by the time you read this, but what I do know is the context that brought us to this point. While a detailed post-mortem of the 2024 election remains to be conducted, we do know that over 80 percent of white Evangelicals voted for him—a number virtually unchanged for the third straight presidential election. But 72 percent of *all* white Christians also did, including Catholics and mainline Protestants. Trump's electoral victory and extreme support among white Christians come on the heels of a significant rise in white Christian nationalism. So, I now bring this broad, too-brief summary of traditional Christian thought on politics to the very recent and local, to address this consequence of conventional political theology. In some ways, Christian nationalism resonates with Calvin's leanings toward religious establishment or Luther's divided "man." In others, it simply reflects an ignorance of or disdain for voices who are often marginalized and harmed by the outcomes of policies championed by white Christians—especially Evangelicals, but white Christians of all stripes and denominations, all of whom have been imbued with certain privileges in this political environment.

Christian Nationalism

Following President-elect Donald Trump's victory speech late on election night 2024, a group gathered in the lobby outside the convention center ballroom and sang "How Great Thou Art." This would foreshadow the many public cries of "God is good" and "God is in control" on social media and in churches following the election, suggesting that God ordained this figure to "bring America back to God," and echoing the symbol of the cross carried by the crowd of Trump supporters on January 6, 2021, as they sacked the Capitol. All of this represents the growth of Christian nationalism, and more specifically, white Christian nationalism, over the course of the twenty-first century. Now, Christian nationalism is not new. It has been around since the union of church and empire by the Roman Emperor Constantine in the fourth century. It has existed in some form throughout all of US history, with resonances in the Social Gospel, Fundamentalism, and especially with the growth of the Religious Right in the 1970s. Pamela Cooper-White describes Christian nationalism as a "cultural framework—a collection of myths, traditions, symbols, narratives and value systems—that idealizes and advocates a fusion of Christianity with American civil life."[17] Yet, it is easy for progressive Christians to name Christian nationalism as a fringe movement, or an ideology confined to conservative Evangelicals—something of which other Christians are guilty, but not ourselves. Like so many other -isms (racism, sexism, ableism), it is easy to distance ourselves from it while allowing its existence in other forms of Christianity to buttress our own sense of moral superiority.

This would be a mistake. While I will at times address the white Christian nationalism visible in radically conservative contexts, we must understand that white Christian nationalism is an inheritance shared by all white American Christians.[18] As in so many other collective sins, we are complicit. Progressives are not immune from the tendency to conflate faith with patriotism, while our efforts to "other" conservative forms of nationalism only feed its growth and intensity. In fact, a recent report found that over half of Americans who attend a weekly religious service qualify as Christian nationalist adherents or sympathizers.[19] The mentality of aggrievement that fuels Christian nationalism is a response to a vicious cycle of grievance in which progressives and conservatives alike participate (more on that in Chapter 7). As sociologist James Hunter observes, the Religious Right arose in response to the political power held by mainline Christians for several decades (though historian Randall Balmer effectively argues that it arose directly in response to racial desegregation and adopted its "pro-life" mantra as a cover), and Christian progressives have adopted some of the same tactics in more recent years to regain the power lost.[20] The nationalism fueling the MAGA movement of the past decade feels like the Religious Right supercharged, though it is important to dissect this reality beyond simple political strategy.

A couple of months before the election, I remember a reporter interviewing an individual at a Trump rally. This supporter explains the feeling of "love" present at such events. I questioned how *love* would be an appropriate description for an event at which the primary rhetoric is vengeance and the vilification of immigrants, the media, and "radical leftists." But the love that this supporter felt, I realized, is the sense of belonging to a movement and to a community. While the potential loss of political power, and certainly the changing cultural dynamics associated with demographic changes—the news that by 2050 whites will no longer have a majority in the US population—fuels this movement, one underappreciated appeal is this sense of belonging, especially for males who do not have such outlets elsewhere.

Yet, as research shows, this is a sense of belonging centered on grievance, what political philosopher Wendy Brown has called "wounded attachments" and "injured identities." People become so heavily invested in their own woundedness and marginalization, exclusion and subordination, that these become critical to their sense of identity, for reasons real or imaginary and even just anticipated. The effect of wounded attachments is to create a sense of collective grievance—and camaraderie within that grievance—so great that it limits these groups' ability to imagine any future that overcomes the injuries.[21] In the case of MAGA Christian Nationalists, concerns about cultural and racial change converge with a sense of communion with those who share those concerns. It also requires the development of a group's identity to be contrasted with an enemy, real or perceived. Grievance and revenge become a central source of meaning—a *raison d'être*—for those who understand themselves to be the victims.

Hunter, drawing on his work on the history of culture wars, asks if this must be so—must injury always lead to a condition of *"injured identity?"*[22] To answer, he turns to the counter-example of the civil rights movement. Black people did not suffer injury in silence, and their marginalization did, in fact, galvanize their sense of collective identity. But it also propelled them to action. This action was not a nihilistic cycle of revenge or perpetual grievance. Instead, they came together, in houses of worship, civic institutions, and places of education to plan protests and civil disobedience, voter registration drives, and mass meetings. As Hunter concludes, *"blessed were the organized."* Their disenfranchisement led them toward inclusion, not into the isolation of grievance. For them, reckoning meant "a day when your grievances would be resolved through enfranchisement" achieved through a process of politically organizing across differences.

Hunter's conclusion echoed a conversation I joined following the election on the topic of Christian Nationalism. The panelists all warned that you cannot argue someone out of Christian Nationalism, nor can you "out-Bible" them. The only path forward, they said, was listening to the reasons and struggles of the aggrieved, as difficult as that might be when we don't perceive those injuries to be grounded in reality. Still, these experts insisted we approach Christian Nationalists not as enemies but truly attempt to understand what drew them to this ideology. Theologian and activist Jonathan Wilson-Hartgrove responded that this advice on taking a personal, individual approach sounded a lot like the collective work of *organizing*.

And this brings us back to how I began the chapter, with grassroots organizing and Ella Baker. This appeal to organizing as an antidote to a politics of grievance is a form of political engagement consistent with a communitarian virtue ethics of liberation. Liberation always requires advocacy; this is incumbent especially upon Christians with privilege who may have persuasion over political authorities. Liberation may also require revolution—a topic I take up in Chapter 5. But for privileged Christians, wondering how to fit into a faithful political process that seeks justice and liberation for the oppressed, the inclusive and mutual work of political organizing provides a means of advocacy that aligns with all the elements of a communitarian virtue ethic of liberation outlined in Part I.

Ella Baker and Community Organizing

There exist several successful models of faith-based organizing, the IAF being the most prominent, founded by a young Jewish man from Chicago named Saul Alinsky. While this contemporary model likely presents the best practical option for privileged Christians and their congregations to engage in direct political action alongside those most impacted by harmful policies, there has been much written on a theology of organizing, especially drawing on the strategy and philosophy of the IAF. (I will include some of those sources in the notes.[23]) I want to do something slightly askew and, drawing on Hunter's appeal to the civil rights movement, focus on the organizing strategy of one figure—especially as one whose philosophy was mixed and molded in the church. As a Black Baptist woman, Ella Baker's model of organizing not only shaped much of the contemporary strategy of organizations like IAF but also embodies the formative, communal, and liberatory elements of Christian ethics. I see Baker's organizing as a model for privileged Christians seeking liberation for others and themselves.

Ella Baker was the behind-the-scenes organizer who bound the Black freedom struggle together. She worked for numerous civil rights organizations and attempted to make them all more democratic and egalitarian. According to her friend and biographer, Joanne Grant, "Her always present desire [was] to form a grassroots organization that would nurture local leadership and become a base for genuine local participation in politics."[24] While she maintained church membership into the late 1950s at least, and a scriptural imagination consistently informed her writing and praxis, her interactions with male clergy leaders in the struggle led her to resist the hierarchical and patriarchal nature of the church, and her time in Harlem unfurled her perspective toward radical ideas. Still, it's impossible not to see that egalitarian congregationalist foundation (Baptist polity, I say) in her work. In a rarely recorded speech during the heart of the movement, Baker proclaimed:

> In order for us as poor and oppressed people to become a part of a society that is meaningful, the system under which we now exist has to be radically changed.... One of the guiding principles has to be that we cannot lead a struggle that involves masses of people without identifying with the people and without getting the people to understand what their potentials are, what their strengths are.[25]

Systemic injustice can only be effectively challenged by grassroots action by those most impacted. According to Barbara Ransby, Baker understood that the strength of an organization grew from the bottom up, not the top down.[26] Thus she continually bristled at the singular leadership style of King and other ministers and chose to focus instead on local leaders and, especially, local people who were not yet leaders but in whom she saw potential. "I believe firmly," Baker said, "in the right of the people who were under the heel to be the ones to decide what action they were going to take to get [out] from under their oppression."[27] Her organizing approach focused on how ordinary local people might become leaders to transform their own communities.[28] In the understanding of the Black feminist tradition, "The purpose of leadership is to build more leadership."[29] Ransby continues, "Baker's political philosophy emphasized the importance of tapping oppressed communities for their own knowledge, strength, and leadership in constructing models for social change."[30] As Aaron Stauffer observes of the practice of organizing, "ordinary people are participants in whatever expertise amounts to, and they come together to solve their problems together."[31] She understood the collective wisdom that resided in poor and oppressed communities, and for her, self-determination was "the democratic idea that an oppressed group, class, or community, had the right to determine the nature of the fight to end its oppression."[32] Yet, this was not simply a matter of empathy or morality, but of efficacy; these communities would be more effective agents of their own change. Baker's emphasis on developing local, indigenous leadership "sprang from her understanding of political psychology," suggests political theorist Mie Inouye. "She thought that people made political decisions primarily based on personal relationships, which developed through interaction over long periods, within particular bounded communities."[33] People had the relationships and motivation; they simply needed to be given the skills, information, and opportunity to lead themselves. This approach is best summarized in the title she gave to her local leadership conferences: "Give the People Light and They Will Find the Way"—a line taken from one of her childhood church hymns.

Considering a practical example of this: while reflecting on the SCLC's boycott in Montgomery, she criticized the focus on King and lamented a missed opportunity to develop local leaders. She spoke of a nurse who was at a demonstration outside the jail where King was detained: "These were women who had demonstrated a kind of dedication, and who had enough intelligence, and had enough contacts with other people to . . . help move people along." The nurse "could have been integrated into a program and her talents could have been developed." But, she regretted, "no role was provided for them."[34] Baker would ensure that this did not happen in future campaigns.

She dismissed the assumption "that being a leader meant that you were separate and apart from the masses . . . and that your responsibility to the people was to represent them. This means that the people were never given a sense of their own values."[35] According to her co-organizers, when visiting local communities, Baker would begin conversations with local leaders and ordinary folk alike by asking: "What are the things taking place in our community that we would like to see changed? What is one thing can we be relatively certain we will be able to accomplish in a certain period of time?"[36] Similarly, reports of the 1960 conference with student sit-in leaders that would launch the student-led SNCC organization detail Baker as "listening patiently," "asking questions," and "warning against dogmatism."[37] Her strategy of analyzing a local situation was to ask probing questions of those most impacted, and listening to others was her path to empowering them. She wanted to create a safe space in which everyone felt comfortable speaking, and she tried to amplify the wisdom in everyone's opinion. According to Ransby,

"She interrupted only to make sure that others were allowed to speak and that the more confident speakers were made to listen." Her friend and co-organizer John Lewis notes, "Before we ever got around to saying what we had to say, we listened. And in the process, we built up both their trust in us and their confidence in themselves."[38]

Organizing, when done well, automatically breaks down privilege because it champions issues impacting the most vulnerable and asks those with privilege to affirm their values and vision. Pastors of big steeple churches and business leaders rub elbows with corner store workers and listen to their concerns, empowering those excluded from the political process toward self-determination. Baker often attempted to recruit more low-income individuals, in fact, by even sending organizers into pool rooms and taverns.[39] Similar to the pedagogical theory of Paulo Freire, Baker's organizing offered a "pedagogy forged not for, but with the oppressed in their struggle to regain their humanity," a more egalitarian model, invested in the concrete situation of the oppressed.[40] Political theorist, Romand Coles, writes that organizing is a response to the lives of those most impacted by injustice that allows their leadership to emerge.[41] And according to Ransby, this was especially true in Baker's model. There was no predetermined blueprint. It required an "organic interaction" between the people involved and their lived experiences and concrete realities. In a 1962 report on her work with the YWCA in Mississippi, Baker used agricultural metaphors to describe her work of grassroots organizing and developing indigenous leaders. Recruiting and orienting new activists was "planting the first seed." The first political activity among the YWCA women—desegregation sit-ins—was using "the blade." Then the development of local leaders to carry on the work themselves was when "the full corn appears."[42]

Tending the garden is a great metaphor for privileged Christians considering how to approach political engagement. It implies active care for things close at hand, looking after one another, and cultivating the best in everyone. It puts the needs of the most vulnerable among us first. As Baker's ecclesial formation shaped her grassroots organizing commitments, a communitarian virtue ethics of liberation shapes a vision much like hers. Her theory and practice of organizing can be understood as a communal formation into life for the sake of the liberation of others, structured by practices that cultivate particular communal virtues, while being led by those most impacted by structural injustice. Just as a virtue model of ethical formation works to create the character of a community such that it already knows how to respond when a moral crisis arises, so too organizing cultivates a culture of trust within a community such that it is prepared for a social or political crisis long before it arises, and already knows how to respond. Community organizing utlizes this model of formation to seek the liberation of the most marginalized and oppressed, and in so doing, liberates privileged Christians from the shackles of our privilege. Through Baker, we sit at the feet of a great teacher who proclaimed a vision of Christian politics of liberation that challenges both quietism and nationalism.

We stand on the shoulders of a great cloud of political witnesses: scholars, activists, and revolutionaries like Augustine, Luther, Gutiérrez, Bonhoeffer, and Baker, all calling us to a better way and a more faithful politics. Remember, for Augustine, we do not shy away from our deepest commitments, nor from political, perhaps even partisan, activities. But we can do so only so long as we understand that we are directing them to a different, higher end. To paraphrase words from the prophet Jeremiah to the Hebrews in exile: "seek the peace of the city you are in [and don't forget to challenge its authorities] and pray for its welfare [specifically for its most vulnerable] even [and especially] if that city be Babylon."

Notes

1 Carol Mueller, "Ella Baker and the Origins of 'Participatory Democracy,'" in *Women in the Civil Rights Movement: Trailblazers and Torchbearers, 1941–1965*, ed. Vicki Crawford, Jacqueline Anne Rouse, and Barbara Woods (Bloomington: University of Indiana Press, 1990), 50, 61.

2 Barbara Ransby, *Ella Baker and the Black Freedom Movement: A Radical Democratic Vision* (Chapel Hill: University of North Carolina Press, 2005), 245.

3 Ransby, 45.

4 Joanne Grant, *Ella Baker: Freedom Bound* (New Jersey: Wiley Publishing, 1998), 192; Baker, 1969 speech at the Institute of the Black World.

5 Alexis de Tocqueville, *Democracy in America*, trans. Gerald Bevan (London: Penguin Books, 2003), 336–42.
6 Emilie Townes, *Womanist Ethics and the Cultural Production of Evil* (Basingstoke, UK: Palgrave MacMillan, 2007), 113.
7 Robert Putnam and David Campbell, *American Grace: How Religion Divides and Unites Us* (New York: Simon & Schuster, 2012).
8 Gustavo Gutiérrez, *A Theology of Liberation: History, Politics and Salvation* (Maryknoll, NY: Orbis Books, 1988, orig. 1973), 132–3.
9 N.T. Wright, *How God Became King: The Forgotten Story of the Gospels* (San Francisco: HarperOne, 2016), 187.
10 Willie Jennings, *The Christian Imagination* (New Haven, CT: Yale University Press, 2011), 274.
11 Augustine, *City of God*, ed. R.W. Dyson (Cambridge, UK: Cambridge University Press, 1998), 19.24.
12 Luther, "On Temporal Authority," in *From Irenaus to Grotius: A Sourcebook in Christian Political Thought*, ed. Oliver O'Donovan and Joan Lockwood O'Donovan (Grand Rapids, MI: Eerdmans Publishing, 1999), 587.
13 Luther, *On Christian Liberty*, trans. W.A. Lambert (Minneapolis, MN: Fortress Press, 2003), 3.
14 Luther, "On Temporal Authority," 589.
15 See John Calvin, *Institutes of the Christian Religion*, ed. John T. McNeill, trans. Ford Lewis Battles (Louisville, KY: Westminster Press, 1960), Book 4, Chapter 20: 1485–521.
16 Norris and Sam Speers, *Kingdom Politics: A New Political Imagination for Today's Church* (New York: Cascade Books, 2015).
17 Pamela Cooper-White, *The Psychology of Nationalism: Why People Are Drawn in and How to Talk Across the Divide* (Minneapolis, MN: Fortress Press, 2022), 13.
18 John Fanestil, *American Heresy: The Roots and Reach of White Christian Nationalism* (Minneapolis, MN: Fortress Press, 2023).
19 PRRI American Values Atlas, 2024: https://www.prri.org/research/christian-nationalism-across-all-50-states-insights-from-prris-2024-american-values-atlas/.
20 Randall Balmer, "The Real Origins of the Religious Right," *Politico* (May 2014): https://www.politico.com/magazine/story/2014/05/religious-right-real-origins-107133/.
21 Wendy Brown, *States of Injury* (Princeton, NJ: Princeton University Press, 1995), 70.

22 James Davidson Hunter, "Nihilism's Grip on American Democracy," *The Hedgehog Review* 26, no. 3 (Fall 2024): 10–23.

23 Jeffrey Stout, *Blessed are the Organized: Grassroots Democracy in America* (Princeton: Princeton University Press, 2012); Luke Bretherton, *Resurrecting Democracy: Faith, Citizenship, and the Politics of a Common Life* (Cambridge, UK: Cambridge University Press, 2014); Aaron Stauffer, *Listening to the Spirit: The Radical Social Gospel, Sacred Value, and Broad-based Community Organizing* (New York: Oxford University Press, 2024).

24 Grant, 217.

25 Grant, 192.

26 Ransby, 139.

27 Ransby, 195.

28 Ransby, 113.

29 Patricia Hill Collins, *Black Feminist Thought* (Milton Park, UK: Routledge Press, 1999), 157.

30 Ransby, 362.

31 Aaron Stauffer, "The Theologically Trained Organizer," *The Christian Century* (February 2024), from *Listening to the Spirit: The Radical Social Gospel, Sacred Value, and Broad-Based Community Organizing.*

32 Ransby, 300.

33 Mie Inouye, "Starting with People Where They Are: Ella Baker's Theory of Political Organizing," *American Political Science Review* 116, no. 2 (2022): 533–46, 541.

34 Grant, 108.

35 Grant, 228, 231.

36 Grant, 54.

37 Charles Payne, *I've Got the Light of Freedom: The Organizing Tradition and the Mississippi Freedom Struggle* (Berkeley: University of California Press, 2007), 97.

38 Ransby, 362; Lewis quoted in Ransby, 282.

39 Charles Payne, "Ella Baker and Models of Social Change," *Signs* 14, no. 4 (Summer, 1989): 885–99, 888.

40 Paulo Freier, *Pedagogy of the Oppressed* (London: Bloomsbury, 2012), 48, 79.

41 Romand Coles and Stanley Hauerwas, *Christianity, Democracy, and the Radical Ordinary: Conversations Between a Radical Democrat and a Christian* (Eugene, OR: Cascade Books, 2008), 58.

42 Ransby, 130, 260–1.

5

War

Introduction: The Christmas Truce

In his book, *The Truce of God,* Rowan Williams tells the story of the Christmas Truce of 1914.[1] Just five months into the beginning of what would become the First World War, British and German troops stationed along the Western Front ceased their firing and shelling on Christmas Eve, unofficially and without coordination. Instead of shooting, they began singing Christmas carols to each other across enemy lines. On Christmas Day, soldiers from both sides emerged from their trenches, walked across No Man's Land, greeted one another, shook hands, and even exchanged gifts. Some reports indicate that the two sides shared in a friendly soccer match. The idea for this holiday truce was proposed earlier in the month by Pope Benedict XV, though it was initially disregarded by generals on either side. Still, when the time came, the liturgical calendar triumphed over the ways of war, and the Christian holiday generated a respite of peace. Then, as the holiday cheer faded over the following days, the soldiers who had wished one another a Merry Christmas one day set about attempting to kill and maim one another the next. In this one story, we witness the complicated, uneasy history of the relationship between Christianity, peace, and warfare.

The primary lens through which Christian theologians and scholars have considered Christianity's relationship to conflict has been the Just War Tradition, at least since Christians first gained political power with the conversion of Roman Emperor Constantine in 312. Most adherents of the just war thread contend that warfare is a morally neutral political act itself that can be used in morally just and unjust ways. There are some, like Augustine and Martin Luther, who argue that it can be a morally positive act of love toward and in defense of your neighbor. Other prominent theologians, like Reinhold Niebuhr, believe it is always tragic but sometimes necessary. And others, like most Anabaptists, believe that Christians should never take up arms—a commitment to Christian pacifism.

In this chapter, I will briefly outline these perspectives on war and their distinctions, but with a focus on an emerging convergence in the last forty or so years between pacifism and Christian just war theory. In doing so, I argue that we ought not to see these as two opposite commitments (though for some scholars and in some variations they obviously are) but as differences along a spectrum with a set of common ethical commitments. Lisa Cahill, perhaps the preeminent contemporary theologian of just war theory, alludes to a common "presumption against war," first addressed in the US Catholic Bishops' pastoral letter, *The Challenge of Peace*.[2] I contend that a communitarian virtue ethic of liberation welcomes this convergence and champions such a presumption. But also, I want to provide a bit of theological background to this, flesh it out, and then conclude with what I perceive as the most significant theological challenge to this growing common presumption against war.

Before jumping in, however, it remains a conviction of the approach of this book to name my own perspective as author. I write this chapter on Christianity and violence as one committed to nonviolence. I was heavily influenced by pacifist theologians like Stanley Hauerwas and John Howard Yoder. And while I maintain that commitment as, I believe, a core tenet of the Gospel, I now recognize significant challenges to it that I will address toward the end of this chapter. I'm aware of the ways my own formation as a privileged, white Christian has enabled my pacifism and shielded me from conditions that would require me to wrestle personally with violence. Thus, this chapter will begin with a high-level overview of the just war tradition and pacifism, but then turn to pressing moral challenges with which I still struggle today.

Pacifism and Just War

The Christian tradition has historically maintained that peace is a basic attribute of God, and thus a theological and moral calling for those of us made in God's image. This notion of peace further grounds the value and worth of each human being: as persons created in the image of God, we should not destroy one another; thus, we destroy the image of God itself. Roman Catholicism especially emphasizes that its value is founded on a rational and moral order of society that has its roots in God and is linked to the common good of humanity and the promotion of human rights. Peace is an eschatological, transcendent reality; yet, it delivers an earthly imperative.

Much of Christian thought on peace follows Augustine's definition of peace as the "tranquility of order," an order for him that sometimes required the use of force to preserve it. Augustine adds that the attainment of peace is, in fact, the purpose of war: "Wars themselves, then, are conducted with the intention of peace, even when they are conducted by those who are concerned to exercise their martial prowess in command and battle. Hence it is clear that peace is the desired end of war."[3] Violence could be waged in certain situations for the sake of peace and as an act of peacemaking—as long as one acts out of love in their heart. Elsewhere, Augustine affirms, "war should be waged only as a necessity.... War is waged in order that peace may be obtained."[4] But much of Christian teaching, from Catholic, Protestant, and especially Anabaptist perspectives, moves beyond this definition and appeals to Christology to frame the Church's thought about peace. Earthly peace is the fruit of the peace of Christ, the "Prince of Peace." Thus, peace constitutes an essential dimension of the Gospel, and any debate about armed conflict must begin by reckoning with the Church's commitment to peace.

In fact, the early church was by and large pacifist in its thinking and practice. In contrast to the Roman Empire, and as a *witness* to their alternative citizenship, most early Christians refused Roman military service. This is exemplified in the writings of many pre-Constantinian writers, like Tertullian, who famously wrote that "Christ, in disarming Peter, unbelted every soldier."[5] But, as has become commonplace to say now, with Emperor Constantine's conversion to Christianity—on a battlefield, no less—all of this changed, even to the point, in the fourth century, of Bishop Augustine eventually calling in the Roman legion to destroy the Donatist heretics that were harassing his congregations. Strands of pacifism have remained throughout Christian history, persisting in monastic orders and then gaining prominence once again during the Radical Reformation with the emergence of the Anabaptists, or what we call today the historic peace churches—Brethren, Mennonites, Quakers.

However, this pacifist commitment has been a minority report within the wider Christian tradition. Since the time of Constantine, while respecting the pacifist position, the Christian tradition has historically sanctioned the just use of force by a public authority under conditions linked to maintaining the common good, protecting the vulnerable, or restoring the order of peace—the makings of a *just war* tradition. For most of Christian teaching, a state authority has a duty to protect its own population from violations of human rights, and every Christian has a right to participate in that protection, even if it means using force.

Martin Luther drew on his Augustinian roots to divide the divine order—and even divide the individual Christian—into two kingdoms and two "persons." True Christians, few and far between according to Luther, belong to the Kingdom of God and have no need of secular law. Secular government is ordained by God for the sake of non-Christians, to restrain them outwardly from evil deeds, because they lack the internal spirit of good will to live according to the Gospel. Luther calls for a sharp distinction between a person in her Christian responsibility and in her given social role or "office;" these, he says, are "two different persons in one." In his commentary on the *Sermon on the Mount*, the Beatitudes provide Luther an opportunity to present his driving presumption. Here, he argues, "Christ is not speaking at all about the government and its work, whose property it is not to be meek . . . but to bear the sword for the punishment of those who do wrong."[6] In matters that are "unofficial," everyone should be meek and not resort to self-defense. But, he says, "If anyone attempted to rule the world by the gospel . . . he would be loosing the ropes and chains of the savage wild beasts and letting them bite and mangle everyone."[7]

Thus, Christians among themselves have no temporal sword, yet they subject themselves to the temporal, earthly law—in obedience to secular rulers—and participate in secular authority and its violence. "It is necessary carefully to distinguish the teaching that pertains universally to each individual person from the teaching that pertains to persons in an office," he claims, "whose task is to punish and to resist evil."[8] The command to love your enemy, therefore, does not extend to enemies on the battlefield because war is a secular action conducted by your outer person in your secular office, and Luther posited no restrictions to killing them "without scruple, to rob and to burn, and to do whatever damages the enemy." Luther laments that the commands to turn the other cheek and love your enemy have "been the undoing of many people!"[9]

Perhaps the preeminent American Christian ethicist, and himself certainly no pacifist, Reinhold Niebuhr offers one of the best defenses of this position. Pacifism is of course no way to properly order the world nor a prudent instrument of national foreign policy. Shaped by his commitment to Christian Realism and pragmatism, like Luther, he agrees that these "utopian illusions," as he calls them, do not make for expedient political strategies.[10] In fact, they would make for a very short-lived political program—serving only to loose the beasts yet again! No proper nation-state could follow the law of love and expect to preserve its way of life and protect its citizens. According to Niebuhr, pacifists "have really absorbed the Renaissance faith in the goodness of man," and failed to consider the tragic sinfulness of humanity that may necessitate the use of force.[11]

But here is where I want to pause for a moment. This "tragic sinfulness of humanity" cuts both ways; it complicates debates about peacemaking and warfare. Theologian Shelly Rambo, who writes extensively about theology and trauma, says that addressing the issue of war "involves examining the narratives supporting our actions." The power of war "does not lie in logistics alone, but in the *undergirding narratives* that speak to matters of ultimacy," she writes. "War is not just something we enact; war provides images and symbols that tell us who we are."[12] Pacifist Catholic theologian William Cavanaugh links war to the undergirding narrative of the nation-state. "The nation-state tends to develop its own . . . worldview and a discipline that aspires to train us in certain virtues, to mold our thoughts and our actions," he says.[13] "The violence of war is [often] necessary to provide some [national] unity."[14] (For those old enough, you might recall the way the Iraq and Afghanistan wars united much of the nation following 9/11—to dubious consequences.) Warfare is grounded in a set of underlying narratives that form and train us to think of our primary identities in particular ways, shape our sense of community and belonging—that condition us into "us versus them" mentalities. This is also an aspect of the tragic sinfulness of humanity, and one that complicates any clear-cut promotions of war or of nonviolence. And one of which theologians like Niebuhr are aware. The point of this is simply to say that there are complicated questions and no easy answers. Christianity has attempted to deal with these complicated dual commitments to maintaining peace as well as the common good—when they diverge—with what has become the church's historic tradition of just war theory, a theory that simultaneously justifies and limits acts of war.

One can discern elements of just war theory in some of the early Christian writings. In fact, the biblical writers include an important prohibition of warfare activity—the unnecessary destruction of property or cutting down trees or plants in war—in the Hebrew Bible tenet of *bal tashit* (Deut. 20:19). While early Christian writers discussed the nature of what is justified in war or what is necessary for starting war, it was Augustine who first began to think somewhat systematically about this. Dating to Augustine and Aquinas, the doctrine of just war began with certain criteria by which it would be justified to enter into war—what are called *jus ad bellum* criteria. Aquinas names three criteria from Augustine's model that must be met—just cause (protection of the common good), legitimate authority (an authority ordained by God), and right intent (your intention must be to fight for that just cause).[15]

These minimalist prohibitions governed Christian thinking about war for over a millennium until, in recent years, the church has included more restrictive rhetoric and additional *jus ad bellum* criteria. These are laid out most clearly in the US Conference of Catholic Bishops' 1983 pastoral letter, *The Challenge of Peace*, which was concerned about the new reality of nuclear annihilation. This model shifts the burden from a simple set of three criteria to justify one's violence to a basic presumption for peace. According to the Bishops, just war reasoning begins with a *presumption against the use of force* and then establishes the conditions in which this presumption may be overridden. This recent, rational reconstruction of just war theory in terms of an initial duty not to kill or injure suggests a common starting point between just war theorists and pacifists in a mutual, "moral presumption against force and war."[16] In fact, as Lisa Cahill observes, pacifists, just war theorists, and just peacebuilders share a common value in the commitment to avoid violence (to some varying degrees).[17] For pacifists, this presumption is absolute, and for just warriors, it must be overcome by meeting particular criteria.

Overriding this presumption requires justification now by seven *jus ad bellum* criteria: Just Cause (protection of the common good or human rights), Legitimate Authority (a competent authority responsible for public order and representative of the people), Right Intention (pursuit of peace or justice), Comparative Justice (the values at stake are critical enough to justify killing), Probability of Success (the successful securing of peace must be likely), Proportionality (the cost of the war in lives and outcome must not exceed the good to be secured), and Last Resort (all peaceful alternatives must be exhausted).[18] The reason for going to war must be just (correcting a grave public evil or aggression); the injustice suffered must outweigh any suffered by the other party; the decision must be made by a legitimate and competent political authority; the intention of going to war must be for that just cause and for it alone; the authority must determine a reasonable probability of a successful outcome; the benefits of that outcome must outweigh the costs of going to war; and finally, war must only be waged after all other diplomatic efforts have been exhausted. In addition, the Bishops posit three *jus in bello* moral standards—what actions are considered just during the course of war: Discrimination/ Noncombatant Immunity, Proportionality, and Right Intention in the midst of conflict—that is, attacks must not intentionally target civilians, must be proportional to the attack suffered and to the state cause/goals of the conflict, and must be waged for this cause.[19]

This general framework has now been adopted by most mainline denominations. Even more recently, many denominations, including the Catholic Church, have endorsed the UN's 2008 principle of the "Responsibility To Protect" which obligates other nations, as a moral duty, to come to the aid of victims within other sovereignties if that government is unable to protect them or is, in fact, the aggressor. The proclamation of a "responsibility to protect" seems to be the next step in the logic of common good promotion, legitimizing certain forms of armed "humanitarian interventions."[20]

A Shift Toward Peacemaking

The inclusion of more restrictive criteria, *in bello* considerations, swiftly changing realities of warfare like terrorism, drone capabilities, humanitarian interventions, and intra-state conflict that make deliberating about just war even more complicated, have all led much of the Christian church to adopt a more pacifistic direction. We now observe stronger rhetoric regarding war from many denominations: inserting more restrictive just war criteria; offering greater attention to the underlying causes of conflict, both before and after war; suggesting the improbability of just war and the insufficiency of the category of justice itself in warfare. These elements evidence a new development or shift in position toward pacifism.

Recent Catholic Papal Encyclicals assert a strong emphasis on the responsibility to uphold and promote life in different circumstances. These references include war as one element of the "culture of death" that poses a grave threat to contemporary human existence. Although these allusions are less pronounced, popes have made the connection explicit on several occasions: "war is an attack on human life," "the battle for peace is a battle for life," "war is a defeat for humanity."[21] Emphatic assertions of God as Lord of life, along with the missional language of participation with God in God's love for life, provide a theological resource for the promotion of peace and nonviolent practices. While linking nonviolence and just war as equal and complementary strategies for peace, like the US Bishops, Pope Francis noted that of "particular concern" to him is the "abolition of war."[22] This suggests that war is not a neutral activity, as classical theorists contend, but in Francis's terms is "madness."[23] Contradicting Augustine's maxim, he claimed that it is "never the way to peace."[24]

The papacy has increasingly opposed the death penalty because of the increasing availability of alternatives—less violent—options that still fulfill the same ends. That is, the punitive option of "life" sentences within the modern prison system now fulfills the established purposes of punishment, rendering the death penalty unnecessary and obsolete. Applying this logic to the issue of contemporary war—in which 75 percent of those killed now are civilians[25]—the ability to wage limited or just wars due to the increasing technological power of war likewise renders warfare a less viable option for achieving the established ends of peace and order. While originally intended to be a restraining device, Pope Francis was not alone in seeing just war theory's "value in deterring and restraining actual war [as] gravely limited." The contemporary reality of warfare simply "adapts the theory itself to accommodate increasing violence."[26] Just as the increasing availability of alternatives within the prison system calls for a shift in the logic of capital punishment, the growing impossibility of achieving limited or just wars and the increasing threat of "total war" call for a shift in the logic of international relations.

In addition to disavowing preventive war, Popes John Paul II, Benedict XVI, and Francis I have all criticized recent "humanitarian" wars as well. They limit the justification for intervention to cases of potential genocide or "ethnic cleansing," which the former Pope consistently condemned as a supreme violation of human dignity. Pope Francis hosted vigils, met with world leaders to discuss this, and opposed potential military intervention in the Syrian crisis in the summer of 2013, echoing previous papal proclamations that "violence and war are never the way to peace!" This represents a significant departure from the views of Augustine and Aquinas that war may be a necessary method to maintain peace. It is important to note, however, that in all these statements, the point of contention is not that humanitarian intervention is intrinsically wrong, just that each situation did not fulfill the just war requirement for justified cases of intervention.

The Catholic Church, among other observers, remains doubtful that any conflict could ever fully meet the seven *jus ad bellum* and three *jus in bello* criteria in the contemporary global context. This practical doubt appears to leave the Church, for all practical purposes, in a position of pacifism. One important Catholic document states plainly, "It is hardly possible to imagine that in an atomic era, war could be used as an instrument of justice."[27] In addition, recent research indicates the effectiveness of nonviolent forms of resistance as an alternative means to obtaining the same goals of peace and order. Social scientists Erica Chenoweth and Maria Stephan have argued that nonviolent resistance campaigns are 50 percent more likely to accomplish their goals than violent resistance and also more likely to result in lasting peace.[28]

This reality of viable alternatives to war, along with the fading likelihood of wars remaining just, results in the need to reevaluate just war theory. The Bishops now identify nonviolence and just war as complementary dimensions of Christianity's common moral vision to pursue peace, both rooted in the theological tradition. They claim, "The two perspectives support and complement one another, each preserving the other from distortion."[29]

Throughout this discussion, I have mostly appealed to Catholic statements. Catholicism has long been on the leading edge of Christian just war thinking; thus, I believe these statements represent or foreshadow the overall shift toward pacifism in Christian thinking. I believe that pacifism and the current just war teaching share a common starting point. The two traditions converge at their point of origin or foundation, at least, in that each presumes a default orientation toward peace. In *The Challenge of Peace*, the Bishops concur: just war and pacifism are "distinct but interdependent methods of evaluating warfare" that "share a common presumption against the use of force as a means of settling disputes."[30] And I have argued that this is a good thing! There is a growing consensus around the initial *prima facie* presumption against killing—and the difference between just war theory and pacifism is now less a matter of kind and more a matter of degree. Do you take this presumption to be an absolute prohibition of killing or war, or can it be overridden if certain conditions and criteria obtain? That is the crucial distinction, but now it lies along a spectrum.

In place of the just war tradition, recent scholarship has gravitated toward the idea of just peacemaking or peacebuilding. Early just-peacemaking theorist Glen Stassen lamented the fact that, despite the term *pacifism* connoting an active "peace-maker," the debate between just war and pacifism "focused Christian ethics only on the negative side of the issue: Are Christians prohibited from making war? It has turned attention away from the positive mandate of active peacemaking: what should we do to make peace?"[31] Just peacemaking fills that gap, providing resources for actively promoting a peace with justice and retrieving a true sense of "blessed are the peacemakers."

According to Cahill, just peacebuilding serves not as an absolute mandate against violence, but "as the cultivation of dispositions, practices, and institutions that foster just peace."[32] It issues not in principles but practices, not aimed at the justification of violence but at its prevention. While variations in the phrasing and number of these practices exist, most just peacemaking frameworks acknowledge the following original seven: (1) Affirm common security: one party's security is interwoven with the security of its adversaries, (2) Take independent initiatives toward peace as an incentive for one's adversary to do so as well, (3) Seek negotiation using methods of conflict resolution, (4) Seek human rights and justice for all, especially the powerless, (5) Engage steps to stop vicious cycles of violence, (6) Acknowledge harms caused and make amends for them, (7) Work democratically with citizens' groups in policy-making.[33]

In many ways, just peacebuilding better fits the contextual ethical approach of this book than either just war theory or pacifism, which both impose a universalized ethical mandate on every situation. By focusing on practices, just peacemakers acknowledge that peacemaking efforts must fit the context of the conflict. At times, violence might be necessary as a last resort for obtaining a lasting peace, but often one or more of the other practices of just peacemaking might be better suited to address the underlying causes and conditions of the conflict. For many ethics scholars, just peacebuilding instills the best chance at creating lasting conditions of peace because its practices call for continued efforts to create peace. Cahill argues, "Peacebuilding must issue in social practices that become broad and deep enough to resocialize former adversaries into coexistence, political reconciliation, and in the ideal case, interpersonal empathy, respect, and forgiveness."[34]

Challenges to Peace

Having laid out the current convergence between just war and pacifism, and the turn toward just peacemaking, I want to identify a significant challenge to a common presumption for peace from liberation theology, one that directly troubles a virtue approach to liberation: the question of revolutionary violence by those who are oppressed.

To illustrate this issue, I will draw on James Cone's Black liberation theology. Cone claims that true pacifism is a myth and just war theory is a privilege for those who go largely unaffected by real violence. This charge implicates privileged Christians who live within the security that allows us to sit around and debate its morality—or to write books about it! For Cone, white theologians' insistence on nonviolence is a condition of our privileged position, and more specifically, our blindness to the ways in which violence is already embedded in our actions. None of us is free of committing acts of violence, he says; instead, we are blinded from recognizing the violence we inflict on others simply through our privilege. By living within and participating in systems of power in which this violence occurs on a regular basis, without doing everything in our power to radically disrupt these systems, we are already implicated in violence. Violence is embedded within every situation in which a people are oppressed; he writes, "no one can be nonviolent in an unjust society."[35]

Cone here invokes the violence of an inherently racist society, but as theologian Shelly Rambo notes, this also implicates all of us living in a consumer system that supports military violence. "To wake up, go to work, and to exist in the United States is to be supported by not only an industrialized nation but a militarized one," she writes. "Simply being a consumer, we are complicit in . . . the military-industrial complex."[36] This complicity within broad systems of violence, therefore, entails not only systemic yet public actions of violence like police shootings of unarmed Black people, and not only our (often) involuntary contributions to the military-industrial system, but also the intrinsic violence of the wealth gap and attacks on affirmative action—systemic strategies to maintain the marginalization of certain segments of the population. "If war is a permanent state, a new condition of being American," Rambo writes, "where does this place just war and pacifist discourses?" As we reflect on this new reality, what are its implications for how we try to live as faithful followers of Jesus? Cone puts the question even more sharply: to claim to be nonviolent within such a system is simply to accept the oppressors' values and participate in his violence. Therefore, the question of whether to participate in violence or nonviolence is moot. Violence versus nonviolence is not the issue. The true question is: Whose violence is on the right side?[37]

This same question is reflected in Latin American liberation theology as well. While most liberation theologians also recognize this systemic, structural violence implicit in all forms of injustice, they do not offer a unified response. Theologians like José Miguez

Bonino suggest, like Cone, that revolutionary violence is well justified.[38] Others, like the Brazilian archbishop Dom Helder Camara, who served the church during that country's dictatorship, worry about an unending "spiral of violence." If, in response to structural violence, the oppressed engage in revolutionary violence, he believes this only leads to more, and worse, state violence. Recognizing, as recent social science research indicates, the effectiveness of nonviolent resistance, he commends noncooperation and civil disobedience instead of contributing to ongoing violence.[39] One of the most influential witnesses to liberation theology, Archbishop Oscar Romero, in the context of El Salvador, called structural violence "an unjust situation in which the majority of men, women, and children in our country find ourselves deprived of the necessities of life."[40] Ordinary violence existed like a "thick smog in the air we breathe."[41] In response, Romero commended "the power of nonviolence" to resist such repression, but does not rule out the need for violence in self-defense.[42]

Cone introduced this question in his first book, *Black Theology and Black Power* back in 1969, in the wake of the assassination of Martin Luther King, Jr. and the unrest that followed. In that book, he seemingly condoned the use of Molotov cocktails against white businesses. Later, in his book *Speaking the Truth*, Cone qualifies and clarifies these claims, rejecting a vengeful motivation for the use of violence: "Returning violence for violence must be completely rejected as an inappropriate strategy for black liberation in the United States."[43] And in his 1993 publication, *Martin and Malcolm and America*, he concludes, "Unless humankind finds a way to put an end to violence, then violence will most certainly put an end to humankind."[44] With these assertions, Cone adopts a form of just war theory in adjudicating when violence is necessary and appropriate, though not in any formal way. Yet, he offers a just war framework for the oppressed, consistent with liberationist values, but still pressing the question of whether a member of the oppressive class or race can actually be nonviolent.

This question is pertinent as I write this chapter, with the conflict in Gaza following the October 2023 Hamas terrorist attack and hostage-taking. While that attack certainly violated just war criteria, Israel's response—which killed over 65,000 Palestinians, including over 20,000 children in two years of fighting and displaced nearly the entire population of 2 million—also violated *jus in bello* criteria of proportionality and noncombatant immunity.[45] Palestinians in Gaza and the West Bank have been consistently marginalized and oppressed by the colonial tendencies of the Israeli government, seizing land for settlers, engaging in settler-invoked violence, and containing movement within the territories. In a situation in which a people have been oppressed—and oppressed by a nation established because of attempted genocide—what is their right to violence?

Returning to the anecdote that opened this chapter, just like the Western Front in 1914, there may be occasional pockets of truce, but these are fleeting. While a few miles of trenches engaged in holiday celebrations, for most of the troops, the violence, death, and suffering raged on. And even those who enjoyed the brief respite from violence quickly returned to the reality of death. Truce was a fleeting illusion. And this is the ambiguous reality with which most of us must reckon, even as we have been shielded from the effects of the violence of our privilege.

Conclusion: Living in the Ambiguity

In the end, I don't know if there are any satisfactory answers to these questions. Are just war and pacifism incompatible? Lisa Cahill thinks not, and points to just peacebuilding as the bridge, the constructive path forward that, in some ways, retains the best of both viewpoints. And I agree.

Is violence justified in situations of oppression? As a person of privilege, I do not believe I am in a position to answer this question for those who face oppression. It is a crucial conviction of a communitarian virtue ethic of liberation that Christian ethics is contextual, and I am not in a context that ought to provide answers on behalf of others. I want to affirm and take seriously Cone's claims that no one is truly nonviolent in an unjust world. And so, I'll conclude by speaking to this question—of how the privileged address our violence—by appealing to feminist philosopher Judith Butler, who considers these deep questions and appeals to responsibility in a way that I find constructive for privileged Christians.

Butler discerns a division between formation and conduct. Granting the point that Cone makes—that we all have been formed as subjects through violence—Butler argues that "it should still be possible to claim that a certain crucial breakage can take place between the violence by which we are formed and the violence with which, once formed, we conduct ourselves." She continues, "Indeed, it may be that precisely because one is formed through violence, the responsibility not to repeat the violence of one's formation is all the more pressing and important."[46]

Even granting that a person's formation through violence is unending, as Cone claims, as we continue to participate in and be shaped by regimes of violence and power, a person is forced to decide "how to live the violence of one's formative history, how to effect shifts and reversals in its iteration."[47] The fact that violence produces the moral agent is not determinative of all that agent's actions. I cannot "dispense with the history of my formation," she concedes, but must continually struggle against repeating its effects. In some ways, I think this is the point and effect of just peacebuilding as Cahill proposes. "The point is not to eradicate the conditions of one's own production," writes Butler, "but only to assume responsibility for living a life that contests the determining power of that production."[48] Living in the ambiguity of these issues is not comfortable, but we must not let it lead us to complacency. Confronting our own conditioning into violence, as well as the privilege we have been afforded due to a legacy of violence against others, means taking on the responsibility to repair that violence. That is the practical takeaway for privileged Christians.

We may not be able to ever fully escape this legacy and our implication in the harms it inflicts, and we should not presume to tell others how to respond to the violence inflicted upon them. However, being mired in the condition of violence is precisely the opening of the possibility for living justly in a nonviolent manner. We can take practical steps to liberate others from violence through political advocacy, boycotts, conscientious objection, education, and contesting misinformation. And in doing so, we might not only limit the effects and injuries of that violence, but we find the path to our own liberation. In a world beset by the "tragic sinfulness of humanity," in which a choice between being violent and nonviolent may be no choice at all, that may be the only way to follow the Prince of Peace, to be a peacemaker, to love enemy and neighbor alike.

Notes

1. Rowan Williams, *The Truce of God: Peacemaking in Troubled Times* (Grand Rapids, MI: Eerdmans Publishing, 2005).
2. Lisa Cahill, *Blessed Are the Peacemakers: Pacifism, Just War, and Peacebuilding* (Minneapolis, MN: Fortress Press, 2019), 18.
3. Augustine, *The City of God*, ed. R.W. Dyson (Cambridge, UK: Cambridge University Press, 2006), 19.12.
4. Augustine, *The Political Writings*, ed. Henry Paolucci (Washington, D.C.: Regnery Publishing), 182.
5. Tertullian, "*On Idolatry, 19*" in *The Ante-Nicene Fathers*, vol. 3, ed. Alexander Roberts and James Donaldson (Peabody, MA: Hendrickson), 73.
6. Martin Luther, "Commentary on the Sermon on the Mount," in *Martin Luther Works*, vol. 21, ed. Jaroslav Pelikan (Saint Louis, MO: Concordia Publishing House, 1956), 23.
7. Martin Luther, "On Temporal Authority," in *From Irenaus to Grotius: A Sourcebook in Christian Political Thought*, ed. Oliver O'Donovan and Joan Lockwood O'Donovan (Grand Rapids, MI: Eerdmans Publishing, 1999), 587.
8. Luther, "Commentary on the Sermon on the Mount," 123.
9. Luther, "Commentary on the Sermon on the Mount," 106.
10. Reinhold Niebuhr, *Why the Christian Church is Not Pacifist* (London: SCM Press, 1940), 10.
11. Niebuhr, 12.
12. Shelly Rambo, "Changing the Conversation: Theologizing War in the Twenty-First Century," *Theology Today* 69, no. 4 (2013): 441–67, 457.
13. William Cavanaugh, *Torture and Eucharist: Theology Politics, and the Body of Christ* (Hoboken, NJ: Wiley-Blackwell, 1998), 196.
14. William Cavanaugh, *Theopolitical Imagination: Christian Practices of Space and Time* (London: T&T Clark, 2003), 45.
15. Thomas Aquinas, *Summa Theologica*, II-II, Trans. by the Fathers of the English Dominican Province (Westminster: Christian Classics, 1981), Q.40, A.1.
16. This phrasing is from James F. Childress, "Just War Criteria," in *War or Peace? The Search for New Answers*, ed. Thomas Shannon (Maryknoll, NY: Orbis Books, 1980), 40–58.
17. Lisa Cahill, *Blessed Are the Peacemakers*, 26.

18 Taken from the United States Conference of Catholic Bishops, *The Challenge of Peace: God's Promise and Our Response* (1983), 85–100.
19 *The Challenge of Peace*, 85–100.
20 *The Responsibility to Protect*, International Commission on Intervention and State Sovereignty (Ottawa, Canada, 2011).
21 John Paul II, *Evangelium Vitae* (1995), Available at: www.vatican.va /holy_father/john_paul_ii/encyclicals/documents/hf_jp-ii_enc_25995 _evangelium-vitae_en.html; "Address on World Day for Peace: Peace on Earth to Those Whom God Loves!" (2000), Available at: www .vatican.va/holy_father/john_paul_ii/messages/peace/documents/hf_jp -ii_mes_08999_xxxiii-world-day-for-peace_en.html.
22 Pope Francis, "Message on the Occasion of the Conference on 'Nonviolence and Just Peace'," www.vatican.va/content/francesco/ en/messages/pont-messages/2016/documents/papa-francesco_20406 _messaggio-non-violenza-pace-giusta.html; See also, *The Challenge of Peace*, 121.
23 James Turner Johnson, "Just War, As It Was and Is," *First Things* (January 2005), www.firstthings.com/article/2005/01/just-war-as -it-was-and-is; Francis, "Homily of His Holiness Pope Francis," September 13, 2014, w2.vatican.va/content/francesco/en/homilies/2 014/documents/papa-francesco_20140913_omelia-sacrario-militare-re dipuglia.html.
24 Pope Francis, "Vigil of Prayer for Peace," September 7, 2013, www .vatican.va/content/francesco/en/homilies/2013/documents/papa -francesco_20130907_veglia-pace.html.
25 Lisa Cahill, *Blessed Are the Peacemakers*, 284.
26 Lisa Cahill, "Just War as a Theory, Just Peace as a Virtue," *Studies in Christian Ethics* 37, no. 3 (2024): 456–70, 458.
27 *Compendium for Social Doctrine* (Pontifical Council for Justice and Peace, 2004), 497
28 Erica Chenoweth and Maria J. Stephan, *Civil Resistance: What Everyone Needs to Know* (Oxford: Oxford University Press, 2021), 13.
29 USCCB, *The Challenge of Peace*, 121.
30 USCCB, *The Challenge of Peace*, 120.
31 Glen Stassen, *Just Peacemaking: Transforming Initiatives for Justice and Peace* (Louisville, KY: Westminster John Knox Press, 1992), 90.
32 Cahill, "Just War as a Theory, Just Peace as a Virtue," 466.
33 Stassen, 94–109.

34 Cahill, *Blessed are the Peacemakers*, 362.
35 James Cone, *God of the Oppressed* (Maryknoll, NY: Orbis Books, 1973), 201.
36 Rambo, 444.
37 James Cone, *Black Theology and Black Power* (Maryknoll, NY: Orbis Books, 1997), 143. Anna Floerke Scheid helpfully distinguishes between types of violence and identifies structural violence as the daily inequalities imposed upon marginalized people by intentional efforts to preserve power (Anna Floerke Scheid, *Just Revolution: A Christian Ethic of Political Resistance and Social Transformation* (New York: Lexington Books, 2015)).
38 Jos Miguez Bonino, "On Discipleship, Justice, and Power," in *Freedom and Discipleship: Liberation Theology in Anabaptist Perspective*, ed. Daniel S Schipani (Maryknoll, NY: Orbis Books, 1989), 131–8.
39 Dom Helder Camara, *Questions for Living*, trans. Robert Barr (Maryknoll, NY: Orbis Books, 1987), 92. Cited in *A Field Guide to Christian Nonviolence*, David Cramer and Myles Werntz (Baker, 2022).
40 Oscar Romero, *Voice of the Voiceless: Four Pastoral Letters and Other Statements* (Maryknoll, NY: Orbis Books, 1985), 143.
41 Mathew Whelan, "You Possess the Land that Belongs to All Salvadorans: Archbishop Romero and Ordinary Violence," *Modern Theology* 35, no. 4 (October 2019): 638–62, 643.
42 Romero, 107.
43 James Cone, *Speaking the Truth: Ecumenism, Liberation, and Black Theology* (Grand Rapids, MI: Eerdmans Publishing, 1986), 65.
44 James Cone, *Martin and Malcolm and America: A Dream or a Nightmare* (Maryknoll, NY: Orbis Books, 1991), 270.
45 Nidal Al-Mughrabi and Emma Farge, "Explainer: How many Palestinians has Israel's Gaza offensive killed?" Reuters (Oct. 7, 2025): https://www.reuters.com/world/middle-east/how-many-palestinians-has-israels-gaza-offensive-killed-2025-10-07.
46 Judith Butler, *Frames of War: When is Life Grievable?* (Brooklyn, NY: Verso, 2009), 167.
47 Butler, 170.
48 Butler, 170.

6

Poverty

Introduction: The Black Christ of Juayua

In the mountain village of Juayua, El Salvador, stands a white cathedral. In January 1932, the Salvadoran military executed hundreds, perhaps thousands of poor *campesinos* in the square facing this cathedral, as part of a massacre of over 30,000 indigenous peasants. Despite its porcelain façade, the cathedral is called the Church of the Black Christ because of the crucifix adorning its altar. Charred from 400 years of candle flames, this statue of Christ—transfigured into the dark skin of the murdered indigenous people—stands as a pilgrimage site and emblem of God's solidarity with the oppressed. Symbols and memories like this served as inspiration for Salvadoran priests and liberation theologians of resistance like Oscar Romero, Jon Sobrino, and Ignacio Ellacuría to write about the oppression of what Ellacuría calls the "crucified peoples" of Latin America.

The Jesuit priest Ellacuría insisted that any theology concerned with discerning the activity and reign of God in the world must begin by "taking hold of reality."[1] He was one of six Jesuit priests and two others who were murdered in 1989 by a US-trained battalion of the Salvadoran military at the University of Central America, where he taught philosophy and theology, during the long civil war in El Salvador. (Sobrino was also targeted that night but happened to be out of the country speaking. He devotes much of his focus in his writings to his friend, Ellacuría.)

For him, taking hold of reality means "not only standing before the *idea* of things or their meaning"—theology as abstract or divine ideas that can be applied to reality—but actually joining people in their reality. It is "being among them through their active, material" conditions, a lived theology emerging from within the community seeking after God. In light of the brutal reality that was facing the Salvadoran people—one of civil war, poverty and hunger, and governmental oppression—he proposed that theology must be "historicized," by which he meant that any theological concept like salvation must be understood "as part of an ongoing historical process, to grasp how its usage interacts with, resists, or transforms, the various dynamisms that constitute one's own specific historical situation."[2]

Moreover, Ellacuría insisted that the theologian cannot fully grasp this reality, one's specific situation, without considering the "crucified people." "A vast portion of humankind," he said, "is literally and historically crucified by natural oppressions and especially by historical and personal oppressions."[3] Like the Black Christ hanging on a cross, the crucified people—the poor farmers and laborers long oppressed by state and church—provide a mirror to those with wealth, power, and privilege, revealing us for who we truly are. They reflect a reality that the powerful and privileged attempt to mask, and often attempt to do so with theology.

Poverty is an interesting topic for Christian ethics because, unlike some of the others addressed in this book that generate clear and hardened differences of opinion, most Christians can unequivocally say that poverty is wrong. I mean, poverty is mentioned more than any other topic in the Bible. The Bible contains over 2,000 verses about poverty and endorses practices to combat poverty:

> "He who oppresses the poor shows contempt for their Maker, but whoever is kind to the needy honors God" (Prov. 14:31).

> "Those who close their eyes to poverty will be cursed" (Prov. 28:27).

> "On the seventh year you shall let your field rest and lie fallow, so that the needy of your people may eat from it" (Exod. 23:10-11).

> "When you reap the harvest of your land, you shall not reap to the very corners of your field nor gather the gleanings of your harvest; you are to leave them for the needy and the alien" (Lev. 23:22).

"Blessed are the poor, for the Kingdom of God is yours" (Lk. 6:20).

The ethical differences in opinion arise when we dig a little deeper for the root causes and the best solutions.

According to the World Bank, nearly half of the world's population lives on less than $6 per day. 8 percent, or 700 million people, live in extreme poverty, which is less than $2.15 per day. These statistics overwhelmingly include women and children. Global conflict and climate change are expected to make those numbers grow significantly in the coming years. One in every ten people in the United States lives in poverty; one out of every six children in the United States grows up in poverty, and the rate is more than twice as high among African American and Latino children. According to Pew Research, the wealth gap between America's richest and poorer families has more than doubled since 1989. By 2016, the richest 5 percent of families possessed 250 times as much wealth as those in the 60–80 percentile range. Sobrino offers the amazing statistic that transferring only 4 percent of the wealth of the top 225 wealthiest fortunes in the world would be enough to provide economic stability to the rest of the world. And while 60 percent of Americans agree that there is too much income inequality in America, you rarely see politicians, including Democratic politicians, invoke the poor.[4]

As William Barber, founder of the Poor People's Campaign and who gained fame for the Moral Mondays campaigns in my home state of North Carolina, writes, in light of renewed attacks on voter rights and gerrymandering of electoral districts, politicians don't address poor people's concerns because they know in a real sense that "they were not going to have to answer to poor people on Election Day."[5] The focus is always on the middle class—the poor, once again, are rendered invisible. When politicians and those with privilege do see poor people, though, they are often viewed with suspicion. Our cherished belief in meritocracy and unquenchable belief in the equality of the American Dream lead us to assume they are the causes of their own poverty. My work with a nonprofit focusing on financial empowerment only confirms this assumption among most people with financial means. Poverty is the result of vice, of one's own sin, even. As capitalism trains us to believe, the poor could simply pull themselves up by their own bootstraps if they were only motivated enough to do so. But all of this misses the key reality that liberation theology identifies: "Poverty is neither innocent nor natural; it is produced."[6]

Capitalism and Consumerism

This reality suggests the importance of taking a step back to examine what contributes to the production of poverty today. There are many structural causes of and interrelated systemic contributors to poverty, including white supremacy and patriarchy. Liberation theology invites a structural analysis of consumer capitalism not only as a force of empire or hegemonic domination in which we are all embedded but also as an almost spiritual or religious force that shapes our values and our desires in an Augustinian sense. According to Ellacuría: "the accumulation of capital . . . makes its possession and enjoyment the principle of humanization."[7] Put conversely, capitalism then also creates a reality in which some people's thriving is contingent upon others' dehumanization. Sobrino claims that as long as the right of property is maintained as absolute and untouchable, every economy will be structured according to a dynamic of oppression.[8]

Free market capitalism begins with the idea of being free from any interference or regulation. We satisfy our desires by being able to freely choose what to consume. This is predicated on the theories of Adam Smith that an unregulated market economy regulates itself for the best results for everyone. In *The Wealth of Nations*, Smith talks about the *invisible hand* of the market. This model claims that the pursuit of consumer desire, that is, self-interest by uncoordinated individual consumers, actually works for the benefit of everyone. Through the mechanisms of supply and demand, the competition for goods among self-interested individuals will result in the production of the goods that society wants for the prices that society demands and with enough employment at the right wages for the satisfaction of everyone.

Consumption becomes the solution for poverty, for the suffering of others. Maybe some of you recall George W. Bush's encouragement after the attacks on 9/11 that Americans buy more to get the economy moving, or the same injunctions during the coronavirus pandemic. Consumption is the solution to people's economic woes. We buy more, which leads to more jobs, which leads to greater prosperity for all. My consumption miraculously feeds *you*. My free market purchasing lifts *you* out of poverty. Consumption becomes a contemporary "loaves and fishes" miracle, turning scarcity into abundance.

According to postliberal theologian William Cavanaugh, consumerism is perhaps the most powerful system of moral formation in the world. Yet, it is not a morally neutral mechanism, but morally deformative. It trains us to see the world and to see other human beings in certain ways, especially as commodities. In fact, people's suffering itself becomes a consumable item—detaching us from their humanity. A hurricane that devastates a community sells newspapers. Or, stories of people dying from Covid sell more advertising on the evening news; those ads, then, drive our desire to purchase the items advertised. It is an inescapable cycle. Consumption is a discipline, and in many ways a spiritual discipline. Cavanaugh quotes a CEO claiming candidly that corporate branding is really a campaign of belief management. It is disciplining our beliefs and desires—a spiritual discipline—to see and want particular things and to act in ways that achieve those ends.[9]

James K. A. Smith begins one of his books by taking the reader through the religious pilgrimage site of the shopping mall (perhaps already a dated illustration, signaling the power of consumerism to morph and shape our desires). The inviting open space, promising to take us into a different, almost timeless time, is "governed by a kind of liturgical, festal calendar, variously draped in the colors, symbols, and images of an unending litany of holidays." According to Smith, this temple called a "mall"

> offers a rich, embodied visual mode of evangelism ... statues and icons embodying concrete images of the good life ... a gospel whose power is beauty, which speaks to our deepest desires and compels us to come not with dire moralisms but rather with a winsome invitation to share in this envisioned good life, to submit to the disciplines that produced the saints evoked in these images. Combing through the racks we find that experience and offering that will provide fulfillment ... Now with our newfound holy object in hand, we proceed to the altar (the payment register) which is the consummation of our worship.[10]

Smith illustrates the act of shopping as a religious act, an intentionally designed morally formative experience, and I think the transition from shopping mall to online shopping—which brings this experience directly into our home or onto our phone for constant consumption—only exacerbates its power.

The Orthodox theologian Alexander Schmemann writes that humans seem to have found our ultimate vocation as *consumer*. "But the truth," he says, "is that the consumer was not born in the twentieth century. The first consumer was Adam himself. He chose to approach the world as a consumer: to eat of it, to use and to dominate it for himself, to benefit from it but not to offer."[11] Consumerism is, in this view, our original sin and remains our principal temptation. It is fundamentally an attempt to tell us who we really are and what we are for. We must remember that Jesus condemned the accumulation of wealth as the great rival to God; it is the ultimate idol, and striving for wealth is the ultimate form of idolatry. Recall Jesus' words in Matthew that the lure of wealth chokes the word of the Gospel (13:22). Jesus sets up an ultimate choice between God and mammon. Wealth and the free-market consumerism that creates the desire for it are idols: an idolatrous faith tirelessly reaching for something that is not God. Augustine begins his *Confessions* with the famous line, "Our hearts are restless until they find rest with You," and this perfectly describes the unending allure of wealth. Consumer desire is a perpetual restlessness, using Augustine's term—a dissatisfaction that always leads us to want more.

Private Property and Stand Your Ground Mentality

There is still an even more sinister angle to consumer culture. Capitalism not only shapes individual identity as a consumer, but produces a commodity culture in which everything becomes property. And, as Kelly Brown Douglas reminds us, property and possession are never too far removed from white supremacy. This is all too obvious in the legacy of chattel slavery: literally turning human beings into property, commodifying bodies and then possessing them. It is no coincidence that transatlantic slavery and capitalism arose hand in hand.[12] Many scholars even link the cause of slavery directly to capitalism. [While I'm sympathetic to this economic argument, as I argue elsewhere, I think racism—specifically a theologically produced white supremacy—is the more direct cause.] Still, however one spins the relationship, you cannot avoid the evidence that capitalism and racism are close cousins and continue to do one another's bidding.

In her book, *Stand Your Ground*, Douglas quotes Cheryl Harris saying, "Whiteness and property share a common premise—a conceptual nucleus—of a right to exclude."[13] Poverty is based on the right for some to exclude others—often violently—from sharing in ownership and therefore sharing in abundance. It is the defense of private property—the defense of capital or ownership and the defense of the right to exclude others from owning—that forms the basis of capitalism, a mentality of scarcity. Thus, capitalism and a "stand your ground mentality" are intrinsically linked, especially bound with the concept of freedom. It is the freedom to accumulate and to defend that accumulation that forms the nexus of capitalistic freedom.

But does wealth bring about true freedom? Does money buy happiness? Throughout history, most philosophers and theologians have said no. Recall that line about camels and needles? Aristotle suspected that accumulating wealth for its own sake corrupted virtue. Citing a plethora of research, religious scholars Charles Mathewes and Evan Sandsmark claim in a widely read *Washington Post* piece,

> When it comes to a broad range of vices, the rich outperform everybody else. They are much more likely than the rest of humanity to shoplift and cheat, for example, and they are more apt to be adulterers and to drink a great deal. They are even more likely to take candy that is meant for children. . . . They also give proportionally less to charity—not surprising, since they exhibit significantly less compassion and empathy toward suffering people.[14]

Another study showed that people driving expensive cars were four times more likely to cut in front of other drivers than those driving cheap cars. Researchers then observed drivers at crosswalks by positioning themselves as pedestrians. The drivers in the cheap cars all respected the pedestrians' right of way. The drivers in the expensive cars ignored the pedestrians 46.2 percent of the time.[15] The study goes on to say that the wealthy experience no gain in happiness as they get richer. The researchers conclude that wealth inequality actually triggers a chemical reaction in the brain of the "haves," limiting their ability to care for and empathize with the suffering. The data seem clear: wealth makes bad people.

The Beatles were right this time. Money can't buy me love; it doesn't buy happiness, and it doesn't seem to make the wealthy feel the freedom they aspire to. Perhaps theologians like Augustine and Karl Barth were correct. A true Christian theological understanding of freedom is not a negative freedom *from* (from interference, regulation, *sharing*) but a constructive freedom *for* (for God and for the sake and the flourishing of others).

So, what does this mean for our habits of consumption? Just as James Cone said regarding violence in Chapter 5—no one can be truly nonviolent in an oppressive society—you can say the same thing about consumption. There is no question of whether or not to be a consumer; everyone must consume in order to live. But the question is what sorts of practices of consumption are directed toward the end of human flourishing? Freedom is not following every desire we have to purchase or consume whatever we want, but to cultivate the desires of God for God's good creation. And this is the contrast of liberation theology's vision of freedom: it is liberation *for* God's work on behalf of others and liberation *for* the self-determination of those who are poor and oppressed. For those of us with more privilege, this requires redirecting our attachments from our consumeristic desires and, as the liberation theologians put it, cultivating a preferential option for the poor.

Liberation Theology and Solidarity

Liberation theology emerged in the late 1960s following the opening of the Catholic Church to the world in Vatican II. Latin American Catholic bishops met in the city of Medellín, Colombia, in 1968 to discuss how to apply the teachings of Vatican II to Latin America. They released a conference report that expressed faith in a new epoch in the history of Latin America: "a time of zeal for full emancipation, of liberation from every form of servitude." This emerging theology recognized its own context and developed a theological method out of the context of the marginalized voices of Latin America, within the Catholic Church, and attempted to think about God and humanity on behalf of and alongside poor people. Thus, this theology originated with both a Catholic orientation and an economic focus.

While Thomas Aquinas was obviously no liberation theologian, even he offered resources that these Latin American theologians drew upon. Aquinas, who certainly valued the right to private property, also wrote that no one should maintain private property in abundance, and if someone is in desperate need, they may actually take from those who have an abundance. For him, economics was in service of the common good.[16]

One of the founders of this movement was Gustavo Gutiérrez, a Dominican priest from Peru, whose 1968 book, *A Theology of Liberation*, became a cornerstone of this new perspective. Reflecting on his experiences several years later, he writes that "Ever since Medellín, the development of liberation theology in Latin America has been accompanied by a continual awareness that we have entered into a new historical stage in the life of our peoples and by a felt need of understanding this new stage as a call from the Lord to preach the gospel in a new way that fits the new situation."[17] Highlighting this fundamental commitment to contextualism, he concludes, "We cannot separate our discourse about God from the historical process of liberation."[18]

The first waves of liberation theology were received with both enthusiasm and resistance, especially from the Vatican. But as Gutiérrez explains, it has consistently approached theology from the perspective of the poor, and for the sake of allowing their voices to be heard. It is a central tenet of liberation that the poor must be agents of their own destiny. Therefore, liberation theology also focuses not only on addressing poverty but uncovering its structural causes—offering a structural analysis that has often gained liberation theology the charge of Marxism from its opponents.

The orienting maxim of liberation theology is the *preferential option for the poor*—this came from the Medellín conference's notion of "preference to the poorest and most needy sectors and to those segregated from any cause whatsoever." Liberation theology seeks to maintain both the universality of God's love for everyone and God's predilection for the marginalized and suffering. So the commitment to the poor, while grounded in social and political analysis, emanates from a conviction of God's love and concern for the most vulnerable, which we see clearly in the life of Jesus: the "least of these," "little ones," "poor," and "poor in spirit." "The poor deserve preference not because they are morally or religiously better than others," Gutiérrez writes, "but because God is God, in whose eyes 'the last are first.'"[19]

Liberation theology also focuses on praxis: that is, intentional practices that are the result of reflection on the way of life of a people as well as God's revelation. Reflecting the link between worship and justice, Gutiérrez says that it is "impossible to separate solidarity with the poor and prayer."[20] This is a theological perspective that begins from the lived experience of the poor and God's love for them and develops theological reflection out of their perspective—from history, from "below," as Dietrich Bonhoeffer would put it. Liberation theology, in many ways, can be summed up by the famous words of Oscar Romero: "The glory of God is a poor person who lives."[21]

So, what does this mean for those of us with privilege? What is our role and responsibility within a theology committed to empowering the poor to be agents of their own liberation? One answer comes from Jon Sobrino: that our own liberation is found in solidarity with the poor.[22] This is not a paternalistic ethic of charity. Charity is important, but not sufficient and can even lead to more damage. For example, a few years ago during his first term in office, President Trump proposed a federal budget that attempted to make a number of cuts to federal poverty programs. A study came out from the anti-poverty group Bread for the World that revealed that if churches responded to the loss of these necessary benefits from the perspective of charity rather than political advocacy, every congregation in the United States would need to raise over $700,000 per year for the next 10 years to make up the difference. The church could attempt to care for the least of these on its own, but that is a lot of tithes! Realistically, churches in the United States can't do this. Charity is important, but not sufficient.

Rather, liberation theology teaches that those of us with privilege must join the poor in solidarity with the goal of helping the poor become agents of their own liberation, capable of self-determination alongside allies who are different from them. In a sense, this is a virtue model of liberation: it requires the privileged to engage in formative practices of solidarity that allow our character to be shaped by personal relationships with the poor and material investments in their liberation.

Sobrino enhances the liberation theology maxim of the "preferential option for the poor" to the claim of "no salvation outside the poor." By this, he points to the civilization of solidarity that the poor have built among *themselves*, as a model and witness, even as a means of salvation. He says that the salvation of the wealthy depends upon our participation in that network of solidarity, which he describes as "unequals bearing one another mutually."[23] The *mutuality* in that definition means this is not a simple matter of giving to them but also receiving from them in a mutual relationship of dignity and humanization. He says that despite having the powers of the world against them, the poor possess something that they offer to others—something humanizing.

What they offer is first a critical perspective—a mirror or light to the world of wealth that reflects back to us our dehumanizing ways. Consider this a call to recognize our sinfulness, repent, and convert. But it is also a constructive invitation to join in solidarity. Sobrino says that this goes beyond a one-way unilateral aid that often tends toward paternalism at best and domination at worst. It moves beyond capitalistic, invisible-hand alliances that believe serving your own self-interest will be mutually beneficial for all. A "well-managed self-interest" is not sufficient to bring about our salvation. That's not true solidarity; it only maintains the same Adam Smith logic, the same Stand Your Ground tendencies, that train us to defend our own interests and own property at the expense of others.

Womanist theologian M. Shawn Copeland, in her book *Enfleshing Freedom*, defines solidarity as "a task, a praxis through which responsible relationships between and among persons (and between and among groups) may be created and expressed, mended and renewed." In these relationships, "we not only apprehend and are moved by the suffering of the other, we confront and address its oppressive cause and shoulder the other's suffering."[24] Importantly, solidarity doesn't erase difference, but recognizes and embraces the differences between contexts, people, and social positions, and celebrates the need for interdependence.

Similarly, for Sobrino, true solidarity is "comradely insertion in the world of the poor, by unequivocal service on its behalf, by liberating praxis alongside the poor, by running risks to defend them, by assuming their fate of persecution and death, and by sharing their joys and hopes."[25] This type of solidarity, as a break with one's social class, Gutiérrez says, is a protest against poverty, even if it means the wealthy take on voluntary poverty and accept risks to themselves. This "costly solidarity"—to invoke Bonhoeffer again—requires the non-poor to become prophetic figures who participate materially with and alongside the poor for their own self-determination and our own salvation.

One practical means of achieving this sort of solidarity is the same type of community organizing outlined and suggested in Chapter 4. Broad-based, grassroots organizing prioritizes the voices and needs of the most vulnerable, including financially vulnerable individuals, within the community. Organizing reaches beyond mere charity work to address the systemic obstacles to achieving financial self-sufficiency and the policy changes necessary to bring about that change. Direct charity service is important; without the safety net provided by food pantries and shelters, many people would simply not survive. However, as a mantra popular among my fellow nonprofit workers claims, "you can't charity a community into flourishing." Creating thriving and equitable communities means we address the reasons people are poor in the first place. This is longer, more arduous, and less immediately-gratifying work. But this is the work that privileged Christians are called to do: to find ways of helping that put us in relationship with those who need it the most—offering not a handout, but a hand-in-hand relationship of solidarity. The work of community organizing is one of the best ways to achieve a true "protest" against poverty and its devastating impacts.

Conclusion: Moral Mondays

I think one of the best examples of this form of solidarity comes from Rev. William Barber and his Moral Mondays movement that has transformed into the Poor People's Campaign. This movement began in North Carolina in 2013, when a series of very conservative voter restriction laws and budget cuts passed the state legislature. Rev. Barber drew on the history of the Fusion Party, a part of state history that I was never taught in my North Carolina school growing up. During Reconstruction, a coalition of poor white people and freed Black people formed a multiracial political party of solidarity to promote policies of justice and equality. By the 1890s, this party had put more Black people in the state legislature than there are in present day and won both US Senate seats and the NC governorship. They passed some of the most progressive education and labor laws in the nation before being violently attacked in a deadly coup d'etat by white supremacists—the only documented coup d'etat in American history—in the Wilmington massacre of 1898 (which is also an event I never learned growing up).

Drawing on that legacy, Barber formed a diverse coalition of community organizing, political advocacy, and faith groups to meet every Monday in front of the State House for a People's Assembly—what he calls a revival. Each meeting had a liturgy of songs and chants and testimony. He says, "Following the testimony of directly affected people each week, we created space in our liturgy for economists, public policy experts, and lawyers to lay out our agenda and explain how it would work." He writes, "Like the old revival services, each week concluded with a sermon and an altar call, when those who wished to make a new spiritual commitment were invited to come forward" and exercise their right to petition the state legislature, even risking arrest. Barber recalls one minister saying, "Never in my life have I seen the proclaimed Word put on flesh and move into such direct action." He adds that "some of us who'd been doing liturgy all of our lives began to realize its power in the public square."[26]

Barber explains, in a fusion coalition, "our most directly affected members would always speak to the issue closest to their hearts. Yet, they would never stand or speak alone." *Solidarity*. And whenever someone from one faith group would stand up to preach, clergy from other traditions—Christian, Jewish, Muslim—would stand with them, "offering the people a visible sign of the message we were trying to proclaim ... learning to stand *together* and proclaim the deepest *shared* values of our faith traditions," Barber says. "We were experiencing a revival like we'd never seen before—one where the Spirit lifts us all from where we were to higher ground."

No salvation outside of the poor. Sobrino closes his essay with the words of Ellacuría—also a fitting conclusion to this chapter: "The great salvific task is to inaugurate a new heaven and a new earth, where sharing trumps accumulating, where there is time to hear and enjoy God's voice in the heart of human history. The poor will save the world; they are already saving it, though not yet."

Notes

1 Ignacio Ellacuría, "Aporte de la teología de la liberación a las religiones abrahamicas en la superación del individualismo y del positivismo," *Revista Latinoamericana de Teología* 10 (1987): 9.

2 Ignacio Ellacuría, "Hacia una fundamentación filosófica del método teológico latinoamericano," *Estudios Centroamericano* 29 (1974): 322–3, 419.

3 Ignacio Ellacuría, "The Crucified People," trans. Phlip Berryman and Robert Barrin, in *Mysterium Liberationis: Fundamental Concepts of Liberation Theology*, ed. Ignacio Ellacuría and Jon Sobrino (Maryknoll, NY: Orbis Books, 1993), 581.

4 Statistics found in: World Bank Group, *Poverty, Prosperity, and Planet Report* (World Bank, 2024), 1; Children's Defense Fund, "Child Poverty": www.childrensdefense.org/tools-and-resources/the-state-of-americas-children/soac-child-poverty; Pew Research Center, "Trends in Income and Wealth Inequality," (2020): www.pewresearch.org/social-trends/2020/01/09/trends-in-income-and-wealth-inequality/#the-richest-are-getting-richer-faster; Jon Sobrino, *No Salvation Outside the Poor: Prophetic-Utopian Essays* (Maryknoll, NY: Orbis Books, 2008), 39; Pew Research Center, "Trends in Income and Wealth Inequality."

5 William J. Barber, with Jonathan Wilson-Hartgrove, *The Third Reconstruction: Moral Mondays, Fusion Politics, and the Rise of a New Justice Movement* (Boston: Beacon Press, 2016), 60.

6 Leonardo Boff, *Cry of the Earth, Cry of the Poor* (Maryknoll, NY: Orbis Books, 2002), 109.

7 Ignacio Ellacuría, "Utopia and Prophecy in Latin America," in *Mysterium Liberationis: Fundamental Concepts of Liberation Theology*, ed. Ignacio Ellacuría and Jon Sobrino (Maryknoll, NY: Orbis Books, 1993), 170; cited in Jon Sobrino, *No Salvation Outside the Poor: Prophetic-Utopian Essays* (Maryknoll, NY: Orbis Books, 2008), 35, 36.

8 Sobrino, 36.
9 William Cavanaugh, *Being Consumed: Economics and Christian Desire* (Grand Rapids, MI: Eerdmans Publishing, 2008), 34, 47.
10 James K.A. Smith, *Desiring the Kingdom: Worship, Worldview, and Cultural Formation* (Ada, MN: Baker Academic, 2009), 21–2.
11 Alexander Schmemann, *Of Water and the Spirit* (Crestwood, NY: St. Vladimir's Seminary Press, 1974), 96.
12 See Edward. E. Baptist, *The Half Has Never Been Told: Slavery and the Making of American Capitalism* (New York: Basic Books, 2014).
13 Kelly Brown Douglas, *Stand Your Ground: Black Bodies and the Justice of God* (Maryknoll, NY: Orbis Books, 2015), 41; quoting Cheryl I. Harris, "Whiteness as Property," *Harvard Law Review* 106, no. 8 (June 1993): 1714.
14 Charles Mathewes and Evan Sandsmark, "Being Rich May be Fun in the Short Term, but Studies Suggest it isn't Good for You," *Washington Post* (July 28, 2017).
15 Michael Lewis, "Extreme Wealth Is Bad for Everyone—Especially the Wealthy," *New Republic* (November 12, 2014).
16 Thomas Aquinas, *Summa Theologica*, II-II.66.7 (Westminster: Christian Classics, 1981).
17 Gustavo Gutiérrez, "Introduction: Expanding the View," in *A Theology of Liberation*, 15th Anniversary Edition (Maryknoll, NY: Orbis Books, 1988), xviii.
18 Gutiérrez, xviii.
19 Gutiérrez, xxv, xxviii.
20 Gutiérrez, xxxii.
21 Quoted, Sobrino, 26.
22 Sobrino, 63.
23 Sobrino, 63.
24 M. Shawn Copeland, *Enfleshing Freedom: Body, Race, and Being* (Minneapolis, MN: Fortress Press, 2010), 94, 95
25 Sobrino, 69.
26 Barber, 105, 106.

7

Patriarchy

Introduction: Every Man's Battle

As he takes the stage for the weekly "Real Men" groups at his new church start, Mark Driscoll is flanked by black-and-white images of soldiers, donning rifles and helmets, preparing to storm the enemy awaiting them on the shore. He dispenses practical advice on issues ranging from prayer to sex to spiritual headship to his battalion of eager men facing what he calls, the "everyday war" of Christian manhood in America.[1] Driscoll served as founding pastor of the Mars Hill megachurch empire, based in Seattle, Washington, for eighteen years before resigning in the fall of 2014. This followed an investigation in which the church elders formally charged him with being "arrogant, quick-tempered with harsh speech, and domineering in his leadership." This setback was temporary for Driscoll, who soon founded a new congregation in Arizona and found himself in the orbit of President Trump during his 2024 campaign, endorsing him and representing a focus on aggrieved masculinity within the MAGA movement.

From the time he founded Mars Hill, Driscoll's top priority was training men. Mainstream and Evangelical Christianity have emasculated Christ, he claimed, and Christian men along with him. Men avoid church because they have no interest in a "Richard Simmons, hippie, queer Christ," according to Driscoll. Jesus was no "long-haired . . . effeminate-looking dude;" he was "an Ultimate Fighter warrior king."[2] Driscoll also drew heavily on military imagery in his preaching and writing. He equated the church's ministry to "air war" and "ground war" campaigns and mobilized men to action through spiritual "boot camps." While this war mentality galvanized many men to give themselves to a larger mission and purpose, it also cultivated a sense of embattlement against a world attempting to crush Christianity and effeminize them.

Driscoll achieved prominence in the early 2000s, the subject of many bloggers and producer of a slew of popular books on masculinity, culture, and sex. These were my formative college years when, still a fairly conservative Evangelical, I participated in many men's groups and book studies as part of my campus ministry. Driscoll arose in the midst of a thriving revitalization of Christian masculinity in the wake of John Eldredge's *Wild at Heart*, among other keystones of youth and college men's ministries like *Every Young Man's Battle*. Eldredge, especially, captured the ethos, articulating that all men were created with a longing for "a battle to fight, an adventure to live, and a beauty to rescue." These works prepared the way for Driscoll to emerge with an answer to the masculinity crisis within conservative American Christianity that resonated with many young men like myself: a critique of seeker-sensitive megachurches that watered down the radical nature of the Gospel, as well as of progressive Christianity and the Religious Right that exploited the Gospel for their secular, political ends. Driscoll's message spoke to the deep dissatisfaction many of us felt and offered a mission, a movement, and a purpose that could give our lives—and our manhood—meaning.

It was only years later that I was able to see the way the fear and anxiety of post-9/11 culture factored into this message and the resurgence of masculine Christianity. Driscoll fueled conservative suspicion that feminism was emasculating American manhood, and that had made us vulnerable to attack from a radical Islam that actually ennobled men. It was up to Christian men to defend America and the church (which were often conflated). Driscoll provided a sense of purpose amid a culture of fear and uncertainty (often by exploiting and breeding that fear), and masculine war metaphors allowed him to demand complete loyalty and obedience. In wartime, there is no room for dissent.[3]

This is not a new phenomenon within American Christianity. And it is also not a phenomenon isolated within Christianity. The term "toxic masculinity" has become popularized in recent years to name a growing and dangerous ideology evident within Christianity but also culture at large. In 2018, the American Psychological

Association issued its first official warning against toxic masculinity. The new "Guidelines for the Psychological Practice with Boys and Men" was the first-ever report published by the association aimed at helping practitioners care for male patients "despite social forces that can harm mental health." Drawing on more than forty years of research, the APA warned against the "masculinity ideology," which it defined as "a particular constellation of standards that have held sway over large segments of the population, including: antifemininity, achievement, eschewal of the appearance of weakness, and adventure risk and violence."[4]

"Traditional masculinity ideology has been shown to limit males' psychological development, constrain their behavior, result in gender role strain and gender role conflict and negatively influence mental health and physical health," according to the report. Conforming to the norms of this "masculinity ideology" can result in suppressing emotions and masking distress in young boys, while limiting any desire to seek help. The report warned that this can lead to aggressive behavior and homophobia, as well as pave the way for sexual harassment, bullying, and violence against others and themselves.

The APA also invoked a series of sobering statistics to emphasize that "traditional masculinity," identified with stoicism, competitiveness, dominance, and aggression, is also harmful. For example, despite being four times more likely to die by suicide than women, men are significantly less likely to be diagnosed with mental disorders because they don't "conform to traditional stereotypes about men's emotionality." Men in the United States also commit an estimated 90 percent more homicides than women and are much more likely to be arrested for domestic violence. This has led some to name this reality a "crisis of masculinity," with this murky term naming the harm done to men because of this cultural ideology for some while naming a feminizing—a loss—of traditional masculinity for others, like Driscoll. Both meanings, however, point to a deeper issue—patriarchy.

In this chapter, I aim to address the contemporary issue of toxic masculinity within the broader historical legacy of patriarchy in church and culture. While toxic masculinity names the standards and symptoms plaguing men and their relationships with women and one another, patriarchy identifies the underlying system that births and supports this ideology, as well as other similar movements in Christian history. The feminist philosopher bell hooks defines patriarchy as "a political-social system that insists that males are inherently dominating, superior to everything and everyone deemed weak, especially females, and endowed with the right to dominate and rule over the weak." While most men do not consciously choose patriarchy, it is "the system they were born within and socialized to accept."[5] But, just as the APA report warned of "masculinity ideology," patriarchy does not only cause harm to women, but also wounds men themselves.

Like many of the other issues covered in this book, patriarchy is not confined to Christianity, but Christianity has played a unique and oversized role in its persistence and impact across time and place. Also, patriarchy might appear more explicitly in conservative contexts, but it stretches across all denominational forms and impacts progressive congregations as well. Patriarchy directly names one sort of privilege—male privilege—while intersecting and supporting other forms of privilege. This chapter will show that it is one element of a constellation of privileges and oppressions constituting a broader politics of domination. Like the other issues tackled in this book, as a particular form of privilege, patriarchy names a particular responsibility for those benefiting from the privilege it confers. And, as part of this broader politics of domination, it names a responsibility all Christians who enjoy various degrees of privilege must address, confront, and resist.

Christianity and Patriarchy

Patriarchy maintains deep and ancient roots within the Christian tradition. Most parts of the Bible read like a manual on patriarchy and misogyny: enslaved women discarded and left to die (Genesis 16); the rape of women captives (Deuteronomy 21); wives commanded to submit to their husbands (Eph. 5:22); women told to be silent in church (1 Tim. 2:12). The biblical narrative even begins with God's curse placed upon women for Eve's original sin (Genesis 3). Masculinity often teases out the worst aspects of the Christian tradition and instigates some of its worst moments—Crusades, Inquisitions, and the church's support of the Third Reich. Yet, within this backdrop, it is important to note a few more recent historical flare-ups of masculinity within American Christianity.

In the early twentieth century, according to Kristin Kobes Du Mez in *Jesus and John Wayne*, Christian leaders realized they had a masculinity problem and set out to "re-masculinize" the faith, insisting that Christianity was "essentially masculine, militant, warlike."[6] At the turn of the century, Protestant churches were perceived as "unmanly." Christianity had lost its masculine, frontier vigor and was becoming "more domesticated, more emotional, more soft and accommodating—in a word, more 'feminine' than their Puritan forebears."[7]

Within this context, the famous evangelist Billy Sunday began preaching a manly evangelism, and books like Bruce Barton's *The Man Nobody Knows* claimed that Jesus was not a "sissified," "meek and lowly" man but a "winner." Interestingly, this was largely a product of liberal and progressive denominations as liberal churches sought greater engagement with the world and culture.[8] Historian Clifford Putney claims that unmanliness was central to the Social Gospel's cultural critique. While concerned to counter what it deemed a too-individualized Gospel, the Social Gospel sought to redeem the "permanent institutions of human society from their inherited guilt of oppression and extortion."[9] And ingredient to its desire to shift the Christian message to the "regeneration of the social order" was a concern over the impacts of a "feminized culture." In fact, one of the central proponents of the Social Gospel, Walter Rauschenbusch, sounded much like contemporary Mark Driscoll when he said, "There was nothing mushy, nothing sweetly effeminate about Jesus. He was a 'man's man.'"[10]

But Rauschenbusch was not alone. In the early twentieth century, to attract men, many progressive churches and organizations promoted a manly Christ. Sensing a division between men and organized religion, pastor Carl Case sought to reclaim a robust, masculine spirituality that reflected strength, courage, and rationality. Through chapters such as "Men and the Church" and "Men and Business," in his 1906 book, *The Masculine in Religion*, he wrote that Christ was a "supremely manly man." Likewise, Harvard University chaplain Francis Peabody claimed that "for softness and sentimentality such as characterizes the feminine man, there was no room in [the] rugged, nomadic, homeless life" of Jesus.[11] These pastors decried the soft, womanly images of Christ in art and hymnody, claiming that most Christian hymns were "unmanly" and contained too much "feeling." One group even created a new hymnal, *Manly Songs for Christian*

Men, with songs promoting lyrics like, "The days are evil and forces mighty . . . He is calling for manly workers [amid] the noise of battle, the clash of armies."[12] There is no room for the mushy, "Jesus is my boyfriend" sentimentality of my seeker-sensitive, Evangelical upbringing here.

I've written elsewhere on the ways German churches employed a warlike, masculine theology and manly vision of Christ to prove their relevance and justify allegiance to Nazism before the Second World War.[13] But this was not a Nazi problem; American progressive churches were doing the same thing at the same time. Some men's groups, in order to inspire "brotherhood," adopted military structures, titles, and language, such as the Brotherhood of St. Andrew (Episcopal) and Brotherhood of St. Paul (Methodist).[14] Fred Smith, founder of the Men and Religion Forward movement, based his organization on the belief that "Christianity is also essentially masculine, militant, warlike."[15] War, specifically the Spanish-American War and the First World War, was largely championed by mainline clergy as a cure to effeminacy in Christian men. Many mainline clergy considered the First World War to be a "holy war." Putney argues that this was due to their oblivious enmeshment in patriotic culture during these wars as well as their desire to prove the masculinity and patriotic relevance of the church. As one minister admitted at the time, patriotism during the Spanish-American War was also to prove that "the church of God is not emasculated as some would have us to think."[16] We see in these examples that Christianity tends to promote masculinity during times it feels threatened, weakened, or a loss of cultural relevance. While this masculine emphasis in the Evangelical and mainline church in America waned amid the horrors of the Second World War, I contend that we have seen a resurgence of masculine Christianity since the turn of the new century, as certain segments of the church feel a renewed threat and cultural shifts once again call masculinity into question.

Contemporary Masculinity

Our current context is one in which two out of five Americans think the country has become "too soft and feminine."[17] An article by columnist David French in the *National Review* puts his concern succinctly. Citing a study on declining hand grip strength among millennial men, he claims, "Simply put, we're getting soft.... Our culture strips its young men of their created purpose and then wonders why they struggle."[18] Perhaps activated by the feminist movement of the 1970s and drawing upon rapidly changing ethnic demographics and cultural norms—including the increasing visibility of the queer and trans community—many leaders perceive a new masculinity crisis. These changes and perceived threats to traditional masculinity have triggered a sense of resentment and attempts to defend a masculinity under siege. This is another, but certainly related, example of a case of "wounded attachments." You recall Wendy Brown's term from Chapter 4 describing a sense of collective grievance—and camaraderie within that grievance—so great that the perceived exclusion and subordination the group feels becomes critical to its sense of identity, for reasons real or imaginary and even just anticipated.[19]

As masculinity theorist R. W. Connell notes, masculinity often arises as a tool in response to some disruption of "long-established and powerful ideals for men's lives, that is, to a sense of crisis."[20] And, this crisis stands on two presumptions now toxically entangled: "a man's individual perception that he cannot live up to the ideals of dominant masculinity" as well as "a cultural betrayal, the sense that men are owed something they are no longer getting."[21] Men conditioned into traditional tropes of masculinity perceive their social privilege fading while at the same time recognizing their own inability to live up to the ideals traditional masculinity prescribes. This mixture creates resentment, then, at a culture they perceive to be preventing them from protecting these ideals.

Harvey Mansfield explains that masculinity has always been an *abstract rage to protect*. "The claim to protect is a claim to rule. How can I protect you properly if I can't tell you what to do?"[22] The desire to protect easily slips into a "politics of domination." There is also a masculine desire to protect institutions for related reasons, like the nuclear family, the church, or political power, that also slips into a patriarchal politics of dominance. And when men feel the need to protect masculinity itself, the reach of this domination intersects with other forms of oppression like white supremacy and environmental subjugation, as we will explore in a later chapter.

Perhaps no one has employed this sense of "masculinity crisis," as in a threat to traditional masculinity, better than Donald Trump. He consistently centers aggrieved, masculine tactics in order to garner support, especially from white men who feel disenfranchised by a growing plurality in America and increasing focus on minority and women's rights. In the 2024 election, 63 percent of white male voters under the age of thirty voted for Trump. This was up significantly from 2020, when young white men supported Biden over Trump by six points. This surge included young men with a college education as well as those without. Additionally, the percentage of young men who identified as Republican and conservative increased by 20 percent in just four years across all races and ethnicities, a remarkable statistic suggesting a growing desire to maintain the cultural status quo.[23] Trump was skilled at naming and fostering the concerns of men who feel overlooked and bypassed by rapidly changing societal norms.

But this Trump phenomenon also implicates the church as one of the primary defenders of masculinity, just as in the historical observations in the previous section. In all three of his presidential runs, Trump has consistently garnered above 80 percent of the conservative Evangelical vote. During the 2016 election, Jerry Falwell, Jr., president, at the time, of the largest Christian university in the world, tweeted that "Christians need to stop electing nice guys" and support "street fighters like Donald Trump at every level of government." This statement, once again promoting images of warrior Christianity, is only one contemporary example of Christians appealing to a masculine theology to condone or implore some form of violence against those who still do not conform to their prescribed masculine norms.

This sense of cultural threat to traditional masculinity converges with a cultural threat to the church in America as well. Church attendance is faltering amid fears of growing secularism. The #MeToo movement that emerged in the last decade has implicated many church leaders in sexual assault. Many churches may experience these cultural shifts as another crisis, and as the brief historical excursion earlier teaches us, the church turns to its patriarchal, masculine tendencies when under perceived threat. In other words, Christianity is prone to employ masculinity as a tool for maintaining power, especially when that power is threatened. When churches perceive their power to be threatened, history reveals the costly means they will employ to prove their relevance. This often leads them to praise those who control and bequeath power and to grow comfortable with moral compromise, and it blinds them to the plight of those in need of their solidarity. James Cone's criticism of the American church a few decades later applies here as well. He claimed that in their desire to avoid controversy, American churches "failed to preach and live Jesus' gospel of liberation. They were *too concerned about their own survival as institutions* and failed to heed Jesus's saying: 'For those who want to save their life will lose it and those who lose their life for my sake and for the sake of the gospel, will save it' (Mk 8:35)."[24]

In light of this reality, of a masculine privilege re-exerting itself against a perceived threat, and a church all too willing to join this struggle for power, what are privileged Christians to do? The voices of the marginalized, of queer scholars, Black women, and those outside of the church who have the most at stake point us to an interesting but difficult task. bell hooks, who defined patriarchy for us earlier, insists that we must focus on the harms that patriarchy inflicts upon men themselves. Only by understanding patriarchy and the ways it damages *men* can we hope to end patriarchy. And only by ending patriarchy can we "liberate men" from the crisis they perceive themselves to face. She insists that many men are willing to challenge and resist patriarchy on an individual level, but not on a systemic level. This would require a re-envisioning of masculinity.[25] The only way to end patriarchy, she says, is "by envisioning alternative ways of thinking about maleness." hooks helpfully identifies that ending patriarchy, like so many other moral issues, will require privileged people to embrace an ethic of responsibility.

Ending Patriarchy

Challenging every instance of visible toxic masculinity will turn into an endless game of whack-a-mole. Feminist scholars and theologians point us deeper, to challenging the ideology and culture of patriarchy—an intrinsic element of Christianity from its birth— as the important work ahead. The most effective way of doing this, feminists like hooks insist, is by identifying, understanding, and alerting men to the damage patriarchy does to them. I'll admit some discomfort with the suggestion that the best approach to challenging patriarchy, and the harm it inflicts upon women and the queer community, is by appealing to the self-interest of men. This focus on the damage of patriarchy for men, as well as the focus on challenging white supremacy in Chapter 8, risks re-centering the agent of domination—be it maleness or whiteness. But for a book on how privileged people might join in solidarity with the oppressed for their liberation, it seems appropriate to address the work privileged people—again, be it men and/or white people—can do ourselves.

The Patriarchal Damage to Men

In patriarchal culture, men are means of production. They must continually prove their worth based on what they do and produce; they are not valued simply for being. This trains men to become agents of production rather than relational beings, open and vulnerable to their own feelings and those of others. Patriarchy corrupts the emotional development of men and boys and teaches them to devalue their own emotional and relational capacities. Patriarchy despises vulnerability and teaches men that they have value only by obtaining external power. Thus, men learn to compartmentalize themselves—to mask their feelings, hold them inside, shut them down, or express them only through rage. One thinks of the classic tropes of the cowboy or Marlboro Man: in patriarchal society, men are socialized to be autonomous and strong. "Men suffer due to the silence required from them," according to theologian Delfo Carceran. "They have to repress their emotion to appear self-controlled and self-disciplined to others." Boys and men are taught by example that they should "hide their weaknesses and solve their own problems. Thus, having that quality, they seldom share their difficulties and so suffer in their solitude and seclusion."[26]

Sociologists have been warning Americans about an epidemic of loneliness for a while now. Robert Putnam's book *Bowling Alone*, from the year 2000, turned national attention to this reality, and it has only gotten worse. In 2023, Surgeon General Vivek Murthy published a national advisory, warning that a growing "epidemic of loneliness and isolation" threatens the health of Americans and also the health of our democracy.²⁷ This epidemic and its impacts are especially prevalent among young men. While the pandemic years certainly aggravated this isolation, even prior to Covid, he noted that about half of Americans reported substantial levels of loneliness. Isolation then leads to anger, resentment, and political polarization. "When we are less invested in one another, we are more susceptible to polarization and less able to pull together to face the challenges that we cannot solve alone," Murthy wrote in *The New York Times*.²⁸ Men become relationally stunted creatures, conditioned to act against their best interests.

"When males are required to wear the mask of a false self," hooks says, "their capacity to live fully and freely is severely diminished."²⁹ When this happens, relationships become based on power, control, or contractual exchange. Culture has feminized things like relationships, emotions, and empathy so that boys begin to devalue their relationality and relational desires. Then male intimacy becomes equated with sexuality, and any sign of intimacy is perceived as gay, further leading to a loss of intimacy in friendships. This is part of the damage patriarchy inflicts upon men.

A Masculinity of Responsibility

The response to the compartmentalizing and isolating effects of patriarchy for men is a re-envisioning of masculinity. hooks insists that contrary to many commentators on the current "masculinity crisis," it is patriarchy and not feminism that is responsible for denying the full humanity of men and boys. Still, she criticizes feminism for failing to address the root causes of patriarchy and provide strategies for thinking about an alternative masculinity. The feminist response was typically to invert gender roles, she complains, rather than re-envisioning masculinity itself. We must "reclaim masculinity and not allow it to be held hostage to patriarchal domination."³⁰

To do so, hooks proposes a masculinity of relationality and responsibility, which aligns well with a communal virtue ethic of liberation. "Only taking responsibility sets one free," she claims.³¹ I drew on a womanist ethic of responsibility back in Chapter 2, demonstrating its affinity with virtue ethics, to argue for why a virtue approach to ethics can lead to liberation for all. As a community of privilege, in this case, the community of male privilege, begins intentionally engaging in practices to cultivate better character, it better understands its position of mutual relationality with others (and the broader impacts of its actions), its moral failings (and the harms it has caused to others and themselves), and becomes more responsive to the needs and concerns of others. The same is true of patriarchy: a masculinity or, we might say, an ethic of responsibility replaces the dominator model with a partnership model; male goodness is relationally oriented, not oriented toward power and control. Responsibility means being integrated with oneself as well as with others. When men learn integrity, they accept the ability to be flexible, to embrace change in thought and action, and to not be afraid to critique themselves and hear criticism from others, because they are more aware of their own shortcomings and the harms they have inflicted on others and themselves. Responsibility means letting go of complete control, learning when to protect and assert and when to let go. This is a life-affirming, relational, non-dominating masculinity that defines maleness as a state of being rather than performance or productivity: men do not have to produce or perform to be affirmed or have value.

Only through relationship and interdependency can men begin to restore their integrity—to be whole and not compartmentalized or forced to mask portions of themselves. This means that men will need to learn to feel and be aware of their feelings, but also feel liberated to practice sharing those feelings with others and not "mask" them. This is communal work. Relationships, committed partnerships, and friendships become "communities of resistance" to patriarchy. "Men will never receive support from patriarchal culture for their emotional development," hooks insists. "But if as enlightened witnesses we offer the men we love (our fathers, brothers, lovers, friends, comrades) affirmation that they can change as well as assurance that we will accept them when they are changed, transformation will not seem as risky."[32]

So, what role does the church play in this reimagining of masculinity? It would seem that if the symptoms of patriarchy are isolation, anger, domination, and compartmentalizing, or a fracturing of the soul, the church would be an ideal institution to generate the sense of community necessary to combat those effects. And while it has mostly instead chosen to mimic—or worse, produce—the traits of toxic masculinity, churches have the opportunity to refocus their mission. Rather than operating out of fear of cultural change, rising secularism, and diminishing power and seeking to protect traditional masculine values and maintain its cultural relevance, the church could return to its origins as a training ground for morals, training men in the virtues of compassion, care, and relationship. This may not necessarily occur in men's groups, but in childcare, Sunday School, inter-gender and inter-generational small groups, and its public presence. Even James Baldwin, while leaving the church of his childhood behind, recalls in *The Fire Next Time* the life-changing moment he experienced that "the church and I were one." In this moment of clarity, unity, and vulnerability, he says that he could see, "Their pain and their joy were mine, and mine were theirs—they surrendered their joy to me, I surrendered mine to them."[33] While short-lived in the life of this literary hero who would have no shortage of criticism for Christianity, this moment conveys the deep relationality and sense of vulnerable community that the church is capable of producing—a relationality that challenges patriarchy by reimagining masculinity rather than inverting it.

Friendship

I try to include within each chapter an example or practical call to action that embodies the constructive proposals of the chapter. What might a re-envisioned masculinity look like in practice? What might the church do to enact an alternative masculinity? You recall that earlier in the chapter, I cited evidence suggesting that the perceived "crisis of masculinity" existed alongside and perhaps was intertwined with an "epidemic of loneliness," especially among men. Men are searching for ways to be themselves, to be vulnerable, to be in relationship, the research suggests, but patriarchal culture puts up roadblock after roadblock. Being a "responsible" person is nearly impossible in isolation, as is making a significant shift in one's beliefs or behavior. We need community; we need friends. It seems that the practical embodiment of these prescriptions points to something very simple but very difficult: friendship. The challenge to patriarchy exists within friendship, both across and within genders. But this is tricky.

"In dark times," writes Hannah Arendt, friendship is "the central phenomenon in which alone true humanity can prove itself." Friendship can serve as a significant challenge to patriarchy when it is not based on mutual aggrievement or, Arendt claims, on ethnic ties or the solidarity of "fraternity." This is not the comradery expressed in mutual disdain for a people group, by "wounded attachments," or through cultural aggrievement that fuels toxic masculinity in the first place—this is why turning to friendship as a tool is so tricky. This must be an authentic, rightly ordered friendship that welcomes difference. And to recognize friendship in this quality, Arendt argues, is to recognize its "political relevance" and cultural power.[34]

Arendt is not alone in recognizing the political and cultural power of friendship. None other than Stanley Hauerwas, not known as an outspoken opponent of patriarchy, notes that true friendship is not a retreat into the private realm between two or a few people. Rather, it serves as an alternative to the politics of totalitarianism that seeks to dominate.[35] The political dimension of friendship lies in its practices of mutual dependence and mutual empowerment, if practiced rightly. He doesn't intend this to be a counter specifically to patriarchy, but as I noted earlier, the politics of domination links all forms of oppression, including patriarchy. If men were to embody a more vulnerable, mutually dependent, and mutually empowering form of friendship, one that bears the marks of responsibility noted above, that might serve as a significant first step toward addressing elements of the politics of domination, patriarchy included.

Guido de Graaff, in his book, *The Politics of Friendship*, observes from the writings of Dietrich Bonhoeffer that friendship entails taking actual responsibility for one another—it is itself an ethic of responsibility.[36] Friendship binds one in a relationship of responsibility to the other, while not overriding their freedom and boundaries (or one's own), because it requires trust and vulnerability predicated on truthfulness. "Christians must bear the burden of one another," Bonhoeffer wrote. "Only as a burden is the other really a brother or sister and not just an object to be controlled."[37] All Christians, he thought, must share in the bearing of one another's weaknesses and oddities, depend on one another amid our fallen and fallible service to one another, and offer vulnerability despite our temptation to shield ourselves from pain or disappointment.[38] He wrote, "bearing the burden of the other means tolerating the reality of the other's creation by God—affirming it, and in bearing with it, breaking through to delight in it."[39] This is the ethical responsibility of a friend, one that bears the other with all of her faults and vulnerabilities, in truthful witness to the reality of her human dignity.

Hauerwas once commented (in a lecture on Bonhoeffer's poem "The Friend") that "friendship is the church's gift to the world for redemptive politics."[40] But as de Graaff notes, the gift of friendship has to be a gift *to* the church first—perhaps a gift from feminist and womanist thinkers who understand all too well the patriarchy the church has condoned and enforced. It has to be a gift from the world, accepted and practiced by the church, before it can become a gift *from* the church back to the world. And if the church learns the lessons of history, perhaps friendship can be the church's gift to the world for a redemptive masculinity as well.

Notes

1. Jessica Johnson, *Biblical Porn: Affect, Labor, and Pastor Mark Driscoll's Evangelical Empire* (Durham, NC: Duke University Press, 2018), quoted, p. 18.
2. Mark Driscoll, *Vintage Jesus: Timeless Answers to Timely Questions* (Wheaton, IL: Crossway, 2008), 11, 150.
3. You can find a more detailed analysis of this anecdote in my "The Problem Was Always Bigger than Mark Driscoll," *Sojourners* (2021).
4. American Psychological Association, "APA Guidelines for Psychological Practice with Men and Boys" (August 2018): https://www.apa.org/about/policy/boys-men-practice-guidelines.pdf.
5. bell hooks, *The Will to Change: Men, Masculinity, and Love* (New York: Washington Square Press, 2004), 18, 108.
6. Kristin Kobes Du Mez, *Jesus and John Wayne: How White Evangelicals Corrupted a Faith and Fractured a Nation* (New York: Liverlight Press, 2020), 15–17.
7. James Turner, *Without God, Without Creed: The Origins of Unbelief in America* (Baltimore, MD: Johns Hopkins University Press, 1986), 235; Barbara Welter, "The Feminization of American Religion, 1800–1860," in *Insights and Parallels: Problems and Issues of American Social History*, ed. William O'Neill (Minneapolis, MN: Burgess Publishing, 1973), 137–57.

8 Clifford Putney, *Muscular Christianity: Manhood and Sports in Protestant America, 1880–1920* (Cambridge, MA: Harvard University Press, 2001), 9.

9 Walter Rauschenbusch, *A Theology for the Social Gospel* (Eugene, OR: Wipf & Stock, 1996), 5, 7.

10 Putney, 42.

11 Carl Delos Case, *The Masculine in Religion* (New York: Fleming H. Revell Company, 1906), 120; Francis Greenwood Peabody, *Jesus Christ and the Christian Character* (New York: Macmillan, 1906), 54.

12 Putney, 97; *Manly Songs for Christian Men*, I. H. Meredith and Grant Colfax Tullar, eds. (1910).

13 See my "Toxic Masculinity and the Quest for Ecclesial Legitimation," *Journal of the Society of Christian Ethics* 39, no. 2 (2019), as well as a chapter in my forthcoming *Virtue and Liberation in the Ethics of Bonhoeffer* (London: T&T Clark, 2026).

14 Putney, 85.

15 Putney, 75; Fred Burton Smith, *A Man's Religion* (New York: Association Press, 1913), 70.

16 Putney, 164.

17 Robert P. Jones and Daniel Cox, "Two-thirds of Trump Supporters Say Nation Needs a Leader Willing to Break the Rules: PRRI/The Atlantic Survey," *Public Religion Research Institute* (2016), prri.org/research/prri-atlantic-poll-republican-democratic-primary-trump-supporters.

18 David French, "Men Are Getting Weaker—Because We Are Not Raising Men," *National Review* (August 16, 2016): https://www.nationalreview.com/2016/08/male-physical-decline-masculinity-threatened.

19 Wendy Brown, *States of Injury* (Princeton: Princeton University Press, 1995), 70.

20 R.W. Connell, *Masculinities* (Cambridge, UK: Polity Press, 1995), 187.

21 Allison Pugh, "Men at Work," *Aeon* (2015): https://aeon.co/essays/what-does-it-mean-to-be-a-man-in-the-age-of-austerity.

22 Harvey C. Mansfield, *Manliness* (New Haven, CT: Yale University Press, 2006), 66.

23 Center for Information and Research on Civic Learning and Engagement, 2024 Election—Youth Vote: https://circle.tufts.edu/2024-election.

24 James H. Cone, *Said I Wasn't Gonna Tell Nobody: The Making of a Black Theologian* (Maryknoll, NY: Orbis Books, 2018), 45 (italics mine).
25 hooks, 31, 38. 108.
26 Delfo C. Canceran, "The Construction of Masculinity on the Theology of Sacrifice," *Colloquium* 49, no. 2 (2017): 8; Stephen Boyd, *The Men We Long to Be: Beyond Lonely Warriors and Desperate Lovers* (Cleveland, OH: Pilgrim Press, 1997), 1–15.
27 Surgeon General Vivek H. Murthy, *Our Epidemic of Loneliness and Isolation* (Washington, DC: U.S. Department of Health and Human Services, 2023): https://www.hhs.gov/sites/default/files/surgeon-general-social-connection-advisory.pdf.
28 Vivek H. Murthy, "We Have Become a Lonely Nation. It's Time to Fix That," *New York Times* (April 30, 2023).
29 hooks 116, 154.
30 hooks, 115.
31 hooks, 165.
32 hooks, 178.
33 James Baldwin, *The Fire Next Time* (London: Vintage International, 1962), 33.
34 Hannah Arendt, "On Humanity in Dark Times: Thoughts about Lessing," in *Men in Dark Times* (New York: Harcourt Brace, 1968), 3–31, 12.
35 Stanley Hauerwas, *Working with Words: On Learning to Speak Christian* (Eugene: Cascade Books, 2011), 282.
36 Guido de Graaff, *Politics in Friendship: A Theological Account* (London: T&T Clark, 2014), 61.
37 Dietrich Bonhoeffer, *Life Together and Prayerbook of the Bible*, in *Dietrich Bonhoeffer Works (English)*, vol. 5, ed. Geoffrey B. Kelly, trans. James H. Burtness and Daniel W. Bloesch (Minneapolis, MN: Fortress Press, 2005), 100.
38 De Graaff, 163.
39 Bonhoeffer, DBWE 5, 101.
40 Quoted in de Graaff, 202.

8

White Supremacy

Introduction: Old Orders

I watched as white van after white van pulled next to the downtown church and unloaded groups of white men, dressed in white shirts and khakis, wearing helmets and carrying clubs. The night before, our prayer service had been interrupted by a crowd of torch-carrying white nationalists marching to a statue of Thomas Jefferson. It was now the morning of August 12, 2017, and real-life Nazis had come to town for a "Unite the Right" white nationalist rally.

They descended upon Charlottesville, a city famous for its slaveholding founding father, that struggles with this heritage while continuing to hide it behind a whitewashed rhetoric of progress. In the summer morning heat, they stormed the streets, chanting, jeering, marching. As I gathered with a group of clergy, the protesters swarmed within a barricaded park, their rage rising until it was unleashed in a barrage of pepper spray, tear gas, and eventually a car plowing through a crowd of protesters and killing Heather Heyer.

They were angry because someone told them that they were being replaced; that is, white men were losing control of the power we once enjoyed amid changing population demographics, shifting religious loyalties, and a growing consciousness of systemic racial oppression. As James Baldwin observed sixty years ago: "Old orders . . . have always existed in relation to a force which they have to subdue. This subjugation is the key to their identity and the triumph and justification of their history."[1] They expressed this anger, looking at us and at the Black clergy standing next to me, and yelling, "You will not replace us."[2]

This book has touched on the reality of racism several times already—as I said, I don't believe you can talk about the church in America, and ethics or politics, without talking about race. While I begin this chapter with a story of my experience with blatant racists and racism, I want to address the more subtle forms of racism that lie beneath these outward expressions; forms that even unknowingly give license to the explicit white supremacy we saw manifest in Charlottesville in 2017 or at the US Capitol on January 6, 2021. This chapter will confront the *contemporary* manifestations of white supremacy in the United States—and the church's role in that *today*. This is important, because recent research raises the question: are churches making people more racist? According to political researcher Robert Jones, Christians are, without qualification, more racist in their attitudes than those without any faith commitment. White Christians registered higher scores on the "Racism Index" he developed from survey and interview data—and progressive Christians did not fare much better than Evangelicals. He concludes that Christian theology and churches have been "the central cultural pole holding up the very idea of white supremacy."[3] Additionally, as a result of a separate five-year research project, Michael Emerson and Glenn Bracey found in their new book, *The Religion of Whiteness*, that two-thirds of all practicing white Christians in the United States believe more in the superiority of white people than in Christianity. Even among progressive mainline denominations, one in six people exhibit higher allegiance to white supremacy.[4]

Given this devastating reality, it is crucial for white, privileged Christians to interrogate our own racism. This chapter will begin that work by examining the ostensibly helpful (or at least innocuous) concepts of colorblindness and racial reconciliation and argue for why they only advance the interests of white people and do not contribute to racial justice. Then I will offer a modest proposal for how racially privileged Christians can better confront our own white supremacy and join the struggle for racial justice, drawing once again from the work of James Cone and womanist theologians.

The Myth of Colorblindness

White supremacy doesn't require intentional racism or graphic displays like Charlottesville or the Capitol riot, but only the willingness of those in power to benefit from the privileges afforded to them by it. The underlying issue on which these explicit expressions are based is good-natured *colorblindness*, the self-justifying confession, "But I don't see color." Colorblindness assumes that racism is an individual and intentional act and attributes structural racial inequality to nonracial factors.[5] It has the advantage of appearing innocuous, even virtuous. It convinces us that we live in a "post-racial" era and people of all colors now have equal access, protection, and privilege.

Yet, as womanist theologian Kelly Brown Douglas observes, "The only thing postracial about this time in the nation's history is the refusal to talk about race."[6] Such refusals mask colorblindness's true identity; like the Wizard of Oz operating behind the screen, it is the curtain that hides the structural and systemic controls that reproduce racial oppression: concealing the continual segregation of American schools, which were more segregated in the year 2000 than in 1970, political gerrymandering that keeps minorities underrepresented in legislative bodies, and the criminal legal system that imposes on Black people longer sentences and more death sentences than whites for the same crimes.[7] Because whites have not been trained to think complexly about race in school, in mainstream discourse, or in social institutions, and because it benefits us not to do so, "many whites believe their financial and professional successes are the result of their own efforts while ignoring the fact of white privilege."[8] We form a false belief in meritocracy, that everyone has equal opportunity to succeed and those who do not succeed obviously fail due to their own fault—laziness or licentiousness—a belief perpetuated by "the American Dream." Inequality is explained by many factors other than systemic racism. Colorblindness fails to account for the effects of racism in the United States, including the persistence of wage and wealth inequality and obstacles to upward mobility within African American communities.[9] Yet the true power of colorblindness is its ability to operate while keeping white supremacy cloaked and empowered.

Sociologist Eduardo Bonilla-Silva provides the classic theory of colorblindness in his book *Racism Without Racists* and identifies the ways this interpretative lens enables "colorblind" white folks to interpret, explain, and ultimately justify the racial structure of society in a manner that protects white privilege. He identifies four main racial frames through which white people interpret racial data, emerging out of our racial history and formation—even if we do not recognize that we are using these frames.

1. We perceive that racial matters and differences are a natural phenomenon rather than a product of history—a process he calls *naturalization*.
2. Next, through the *cultural racism* frame, white people avoid attributing racial inequality to biological inferiority but now consider it a consequence of "cultural" characteristics, such as lack of family structure or conditioned laziness.
3. Third, the frame of *minimization* simply discounts the role discrimination still plays in hiring practices or neighborhood segregation.[10]
4. The fourth and most significant frame, according to Bonilla-Silva, is *abstract liberalism,* upon which the United States was founded. The two core tenets of abstract liberalism are the strongly held convictions of equal opportunity and individual freedom. The belief in equal opportunity allows whites to urge equality while opposing affirmative action because it grants special treatment to one group. It upholds a belief in meritocracy that considers everyone to have equal access and opportunity—and thus equal, individual responsibility to "make it on their own."[11] Yet, it is abstract because it ignores the history and conditions that created the inequality, and it neglects the policies that create power differences between races.

These four frames help explain white people's belief in racism as individual prejudice and our blindness to its structural forms. Through them, the violence of racial oppression implicates even the most well-meaning white people and keeps us oblivious to this reality. It prevents us from seeing the ways in which, as philosopher Charles Mills notes, even poor whites are able to affirm their whiteness (or at least receive the benefits it bequeaths) that distinguish them from those on the other side of the color line.[12] White people are ferociously barricaded inside our sanitized version of this history. Colorblindness leaves uninterrogated the assumptions and histories that have caused us to arrive at our current situation.

Colorblindness is simply a manifestation of the problem of whiteness, another mode of formation that we embody but often do not see. Definitions of whiteness abound, but for my purposes, it is helpfully described by Robin DiAngelo as a constellation of processes and practices that "include basic rights, values, beliefs, perspectives, and experiences purported to be commonly shared by all but which are actually only consistently afforded to white people."[13] "Dynamic, relational, and operating at all times on myriad levels," whiteness simultaneously trades in pretensions to universality while also "othering" those who are not seen as white. Ruth Frankenburg further breaks down whiteness into three registers:[14]

1. First, whiteness "is a location of structural advantage, of race *privilege*"—the reality of white privilege.
2. Second, "it is a 'standpoint,' a *position* from which white people look at ourselves, at others, and society." It allows white people the privilege of abstracting from skin color—not seeing color, even our own—and assuming that our access and opportunity are universal. White people seem unable to perceive whiteness as a racial category.[15]
3. Third, it refers to a set of cultural *practices*, though due to its universalizing tendencies, these practices are usually unmarked and unnamed.

Yet, there is a more insidious dimension to colorblindness that often goes untreated in public discourse on the subject. Most often, colorblindness is the presumption to not see the color of minority "others." But colorblindness also names the inability (or refusal) of whites to see the effects of our own skin color. In other words, colorblindness allows whiteness to camouflage itself. Even perceptive whites who acknowledge the existence of systemic social injustice often have difficulty connecting this explicitly to the sordid history of race, rather than simply class or some other social category, and acknowledging that *all* white people benefit from the systems set in place by racism.

African Americans who suffer the structural effects of racism know this is not true. James Cone says, "What is invisible to white Christians and their theologians is inescapable to Black people."[16] Yet because whites have a dominant hold on the narrative, whites define the terms of the conversation and limit its scope. "Most whites do not see the problem of race in America as a white problem," write sociologists Joe Feagin and Eileen O'Brien,[17] because racial privilege is lived, unconsciously experienced, rather than seen. Once it became interwoven into the fabric of American culture and institutions, white supremacy could disappear and operate in a clandestine fashion. But this elusiveness had the effect of hiding whiteness from the very people benefiting from the privileges it conveys. Colorblindness, therefore, shields white people from seeing that we too have a color, and from seeing the ways in which that color shapes our vision of the world and of others. It is blindness to the context of our own racial formation—that is, the ways we have been conditioned as whites to accept, unquestioningly, the benefits of our whiteness.

This allows whites to think of ourselves as universal humans who represent all of human experience.[18] White people "do not recognize the narrowness of their experience and the particularity of their theological expressions," Cone charges. "They like to think of themselves as universal people."[19] Our universal, neutral, and natural pretensions make it difficult to discern, much less uncover, talk about, and confront. As the self-appointed universal surveyor and judge, enabled to see and categorize all, the one thing whiteness cannot see is itself.[20]

Fresh out of seminary, I took a job as senior pastor of a fledgling congregation on the outskirts of Raleigh, NC. The church got its start after splitting from a larger congregation (as Baptists are prone to do) over some issue not serious enough to recall. The local neighborhood was a typical blue-collar area that had become increasingly diverse in recent years, as many white families moved to more prosperous corners of the city. Simply due to our location, several African American families had begun attending regularly before my arrival. They participated in the weekly Bible study as well as the praise and worship band.

The church leadership had decided, around the time I began serving as pastor, to reach out to young professionals in the growing Research Triangle area. They were willing to devote the congregation's resources, even dip into our endowment, to relocate closer to the area that housed numerous technology firms and global businesses. Our contemporary worship style, nimble leadership team, and tentative relationship to our neighborhood reflected this desire and primed us to become a church of young professionals, they thought.

At the same time, we were unintentionally growing into a multi-ethnic congregation, a rare feat for rural, southern congregations. Yet no one ever brought attention to this fact. No one left the church because of its changing color, but no one seemed to mark it as a gift, either. We saw no particular value in multi-ethnic community—social, pedagogical, or spiritual—and viewed the integration of Black families into the church body as no reason to make changes to the structures, practices, or leadership of the congregation. No one mentioned the possibility of singing Gospel music, reading scripture commentaries by Black authors, or changing the leadership team to more accurately reflect the demographics of the congregation. The Gospel is colorblind, the leadership believed, and at the time I possessed no resources to challenge this claim. Grace is universally available; God is no respecter of persons (Acts 10:34). So, I agreed that the racial demographics of the congregation need not alter our practices or leadership structure.

I never questioned why they were so eager to draw in "young professionals" from the local technology and business park. The unspoken—likely even unperceived—desire was to fill the pews with young, upwardly mobile white families. These were the types of people who would help "grow" the congregation—in numbers, prestige, and budget. I don't think this was an *intentionally* racist desire, just unreflective. Nevertheless, both this desire and the failure to recognize an inherent value to racial diversity were based on a theology of colorblindness, one that had its roots firmly planted in the legacy of white supremacy. And I, as pastor, was blind to that.

Womanist theologian Emilie Townes more precisely names this type of colorblindness *uninterrogated whiteness*. She describes this as the avoidance of asking "how whiteness has been constructed and how it is maintained as a largely uninterrogated phenomenon of alleged neutrality—or worse, of being the norm."[21] In short, it is a failure to examine context: the ways that whiteness determines the issues we address, the questions we ask, and the answers we derive from those questions.[22] It is the privilege of ignorance that allows white people to avoid addressing the ways that the particular opportunities, experiences, challenges, and successes afforded to people have been largely determined by one's racial location, and in the case of white folks, likely a privileged racial location. This is what Baldwin was able to perceive nearly fifty years ago, that "White America remains unable to believe that Black America's grievances are real; they are unable to believe this because they cannot face what this fact says about themselves and their country."[23]

Townes further identifies the ways this limited vision contributes to the formation of harmful and racist public policies.[24] When decision-makers do not realize that they have a socially and racially conditioned lens that allows them to see only a small portion of the world based on their experience and context—what Townes calls "unexamined particularity"[25]—and then project this unseen particularity universally upon everyone's experience, then they make policies that do not account for the contexts, struggles, and obstacles faced by others. Examples abound: disparities in Covid testing and vaccinations during the pandemic, the distribution of educational resources among school systems, or, as Michelle Alexander observes, imbalances in the criminal legal system.

Racial Reconciliation

The concept and practice of colorblindness often commission appeals to racial reconciliation as the solution to racial injustice. Today, white churches and many multiracial congregations remain unreflective about the ways whiteness impacts their theological positions and practices. When they do perceive a problem with race—most often identified as racial *division*—many well-intentioned congregations propose various models of *racial reconciliation,* ranging from a simple pulpit exchange or annual fellowship meal to shared mission projects or targeted efforts at creating "diversity." For many sincere Christians, the work of racial reconciliation is integral to their theology and ministry and predicated on a strong biblical imperative. The Apostle Paul tells us that we are to be agents of reconciliation (2 Cor. 5:18-19), and this concept has been baked into our theology.

Yet, African Americans have long had good reasons to be suspicious of white desires for reconciliation. For Cone, this means that liberation must be a precondition for reconciliation. Most white theologians and white churches permit their desire for reconciliation to overrun the self-interrogative work that liberation requires. White theologian Jennifer Harvey takes up this issue in her book, *Dear White Christians*, and argues that the "reconciliation paradigm" has failed. The eagerness of most advocates of reconciliation pushes them to reach for shallow solutions and premature solidarity. For her, the problem with reconciliation is that it rests on the universalist ethic described above that supports whiteness. Whites are trained to see our perspectives as objective and universal, and thus normative.[26] Our colorblindness projects our own particular experiences universally onto all others and imposes one uniform standard to which we can hold one another accountable across racial difference—so of course my Black brothers and sisters would want to be reconciled just as much as I do!

The consequence of this universalist preoccupation with sameness is the often-unnamed belief that everyone equally bears the burden of reconciliation. It places the same duty owed to one another on everyone and entails the same urgency for unity on all parties, despite one's location of privilege or oppression. We each start from our own end and meet in the middle, each party contributing equally to the work of reconciliation and unity. As Harvey argues, an awareness of the fact that whites bear more responsibility is "flattened" into a universal and equal call to action.[27] Reconciliation thus becomes a more costly endeavor for Black Christians than for whites and fails to address the deeper, collective problem of white supremacy.

The fact that white people want to move so quickly to "reconciliation," James Cone contends, is a symptom of white people's short memories.[28] But white people cannot be trusted to define the terms of reconciliation, he asserts, because we have been "enslaved by [our] own racism."[29] Oppressors should not be the ones to define what reconciliation looks like. Likewise, whatever models of reconciliation we come up with are themselves shaped by our inevitable white supremacy, and thus inadequate for the task. Reconciliation will never be possible (at least!) until the white church and white theology first confront the white supremacy that has deformed our churches and theologies and then release our own expectations of what reconciliation looks like in exchange for those of the oppressed.[30] This does not mean that reconciliation isn't an eschatological reality that ought to guide our ethics—that is, a vision of our future peaceable kingdom with God (Isa. 11:6-9)—only that in our present condition, any attempts to actualize it will likely replicate racial harm. And this means that, in the interim, white Christians should stop promoting the task of racial reconciliation.

Confronting White Supremacy: Becoming Black

I know this is a difficult claim. Progressive white Christians have been shaped by the message of racial reconciliation for so long. But one key reason for this is that we have neglected Black and Brown voices telling us that this is not the way. The more we understand racism to be morally wrong, the more we shield ourselves from seeing the ways we participate in racism. We craft strategies to distance ourselves from the possibility of racial advantage or feelings of racial superiority.

In a study of my own denomination, the Alliance of Baptists, a historically white progressive body that has recently committed to becoming an anti-racist organization, sociologist Gerardo Marti observes, "These white liberal Christians demonstrate a deep desire to do the right thing: to love Black people and to be deemed an ally." Yet, in their work to become anti-racist, the desire to "get it right" coincides with a greater fear of getting it wrong.[31] He finds the congregations to be "stuck," unsure about finding a path for acting more constructively and more confidently in their anti-racism work. As they begin to see the ways racism is rooted in all the structures and systems around them, they struggle with what he calls an "unseen racialized religion," the recognition that they are a "white church" alongside their previous understandings of the Black Church or Hispanic churches. Attempting to be a "good white person" creates this uncertainty and generally results in them striving to be culturally competent but also avoiding conflict: continually stuck in the stages of talking, processing, and perhaps better. This attempt to embody a new social narrative as a "white church" trying to ally with the marginalized then becomes a form of performativity "meant less to assert virtue but rather to avoid conflict," he writes. "No one wants to be embarrassed, no one wants to be called out, and no one wants to be humiliated."[32]

In other words, the more we understand racism to be an evil, the more we want to do something about it, and the more we become uncertain about what that "something" ought to be. This leaves well-intentioned white people in a spiral, unable to fully address the depth of the issue. In fact, as M. Shawn Copeland observes, "Racism is no mere problem to be solved; it is a way in which we define our reality, live the most intimate moments of our lives. Racism is not something *out-there* for us to solve or fix; racism is *in us*, sedimented in our consciousness" and institutions. So what are we to do about it?

To begin thinking constructively, I will turn again to James Cone and his proposal for how to overcome white supremacy—a proposal that aligns well with the virtue ethic of liberation proposed in this book. Cone makes the radical claim that to confront our white supremacy, white people must *become Black*. But what does this mean? And, how? Cone describes this as a process of conversion to Blackness. And like the old Baptist Evangelical testimonies of a conversion experience with which I grew up, this process has particular and necessary steps and actions. Consistent with a virtue ethic of liberation, these are not steps to solve racism as a problem, but practices to morally transform ourselves into people committed to anti-racism—to become Black.

White people can only do this, he insists in *Black Theology and Black Power*, drawing on Jesus' words in Mk 8:34, if we (1) "deny [our]selves (whiteness), (2) take up the cross (Blackness), and (3) follow Christ into, what he calls, the (Black ghetto)."[33] The three steps he identifies by drawing upon Jesus' words to his disciples result in three practices, a catechesis of Blackness, so to speak: denying (perhaps refusing is an even better term) our whiteness, taking up the story of Blackness, and following Christ into concrete solidarity with Black people. Let's take a deeper look at each of these steps.

Denying Whiteness

By denying whiteness, I do not mean a retreat into colorblindness or white defensiveness or "fragility."[34] Rather, Cone insists we deny the privileges of whiteness. Any process of conversion begins with recognizing one's social location and history. Conversion entails a recollection of something that has been lost or corrupted due to poor formation—or sin. Denying whiteness, as Cone urges, begins with remembering the ways whiteness has distorted our vision of the world and one another and reflecting on the oppression we have imposed on much of the world. Despite our inclinations to forget that past and move on, resistance to white supremacy begins with remembering our collective past. Cone says, "My hope is that whites will be redeemed from their blindness, and open their eyes to the terror of their deeds so they will know we are all of one blood and what we do to others we do to ourselves."[35] I had the privilege of conducting several interviews with James Cone before he passed. In one of those, he told me, "If white people and Black people are going to be reconciled, they have to do that looking at the lynched bodies, the enslaved bodies, the Trayvon Martins. You've got to look them in the eye, their mothers, their fathers."

The work of confronting white supremacy and becoming actively anti-racist is always going to be incomplete and imperfect. But one crucial way of denying whiteness is to begin understanding inclusivity as the enemy of anti-racism. The cozy Christian belief that all voices matter results in a commitment to avoid controversy—being "stuck" in fear of conflict. Denying whiteness begins by privileging marginalized voices and voices of color and not viewing all voices as equal in this conversation. Only at that point is conversion possible.

Taking Up Blackness

Next, conversion to Blackness means taking up the cross of Blackness—that is, taking on the Black story in all its particularity and all its risk and suffering, joy and redemption. This is not a project of appropriation but a catechesis in which white allies must submit to the authority of new teachers and exemplars in the struggle for Black liberation. As Cone explains, "White converts, if there are any to be found, must be made to realize that they are like babies who have barely learned to walk and talk."[36] White Christians must continually reject their whiteness by submitting in full accountability to Black leaders until our "value system is now defined by the oppressed engaged in the liberation struggle."[37] Taking up Blackness entails interrogating the ethical values of whiteness and listening to the moral authority of Black leaders. This requires actively destroying whiteness by working alongside the oppressed, taking on their values and risks as our own, to the degree that a person of privilege is able.

This activity is best described in theological language as repentance, which Cone, quoting Alan Richardson, defines as a "reorientation of one's whole life and personality, which includes the adoption of a new ethical line of conduct, a forsaking of sin and a turning to righteousness."[38] Taking up the cross of Blackness is the continuous, diligent work of refusing the privileges of whiteness and submitting in accountability to our Black sisters and brothers. This is not sympathy, but solidarity and sacrifice—a reorienting of the self and the self's relation to the world around it, giving up power, and placing oneself in a position beneath the authority of Black leaders and teachers.

Following the Black Christ

Finally, the last step in becoming Black is following Christ into "the Black ghetto." I interpret Cone's claim to invoke the need for concrete, material change to repair the racial harms we have inflicted. This is a direct challenge to the abstracting tendencies of whiteness, often predicated on our fear of facing the realities we created, our inability to see beyond the narrowness of our experience.

In other words, repentance is completed through acts of reparation. Recall the story of Zacchaeus's conversion in Luke 19. After a life of stealing money from the poor, enabled by the power of empire, he commits to giving half of his possessions to the poor, and "if I have defrauded anyone of anything, I will pay back four times as much." This story teaches us that repentance is not complete until it is made concrete by material acts of atonement for one's sins. True solidarity with Black people (for Cone, truly following Christ) must involve sacrifice and taking on the same risks as those you claim to join. Repentance without material repair is cheap repentance.[39] Reparation may take several forms and must be developed in conversation and under the guidance of the oppressed, but in the particular circumstances of Black oppression in America, surely one of these forms is financial.

Conclusion: Theology's Great Sin

Americans are living in a new moment of racial crisis. We have witnessed a rise in racially motivated hate crimes and racially motivated police brutality. White nationalists feel emboldened to march in the streets march in the streets, run for political office, and preach from pulpits. Conservative politicians continue to attack voting rights, fueled by many whites who feel threatened by a growing ethnic pluralism in America and an increasing focus on minority rights. This phenomenon reveals the tight grip of the dominance of white supremacy. The explicit racism we see carrying a Confederate flag in the US Capitol is funded by the implicit and silent support of whites who fail to see the ways we are all implicated in white supremacy. It is all an attempt to cling to the hegemonic power long enjoyed by White Christian America.[40]

This reality is especially important for white Christians to recognize because the white church reflects the same racial distortions and fragmentations that one observes in society at large and appears integral to funding its continued power. Jonathan Tran puts the issue pointedly when he writes that white Christians cannot commit all the atrocities they have committed in God's name and "still expect the moral infrastructure in which we committed those atrocities to remain intact. The atrocities demonstrate that either the infrastructure is not to be trusted or we are not to be entrusted with it."[41] In Kelly Brown Douglas's words, considering the way Christianity has been used for centuries to oppress Black people, we must seriously ask, "was there not something wrong with Christianity itself?"[42] The complicity of the white church and white theology in racial oppression—from colonialism and slavery to Jim Crow and mass incarceration—challenges the very legitimacy of the institution. What is most striking, considering the perpetual significance of this issue, is the silence of so many white churches and theologians on matters of race, racism, and whiteness—a silence that Cone calls "theology's great sin."[43] The work of racial repair is long and difficult. As Cone claims, it requires a conversion.

Conversion is a process of small, uncomfortable steps. In his study of white congregations attempting to become anti-racist, Marti observed the small steps many were taking in this work—incomplete and insufficient, but steps along the way of conversion. "Those of us who lead progressive white churches, particularly white pastors, can call our members and our churches to do actions that are within our reach," he notes:

> giving attention to Black and Indigenous voices; having conversations that clarify and (if necessary) confront choices in consumer purchases, budget and hiring decisions, and signs and symbols we display; developing partnerships with similarly concerned others where the church can learn more about anti-racism. Such actions can pave the way for much larger changes—paying reparations, participating in civil disobedience, running for office, speaking in public, writing to teach our communities, working alongside others to benefit people of color, building more intimate cross-racial relationships.[44]

Visible explosions of white supremacy like I witnessed in Charlottesville in 2017 are only the symptom of a deeper problem. White supremacy not only describes individual actors: Dylan Roof or white nationalist ralliers. It is a system that implicates all white people. The danger doesn't only carry a Nazi flag; it sits in our pews, stands in our pulpits, and occasionally tells racist jokes, talks of immigrant "invasions," cites "cultural differences," or identifies problems "on many sides." The casual disinterest, appeals to unity and colorblindness, and premature calls for reconciliation by many white Christians leave us no better than those the prophet Jeremiah admonished for "superficially healing the brokenness of my people by saying, 'Peace, peace,' when there is no peace" (Jer. 6:14).

Notes

1 James Baldwin, *No Name in the Street* (New York: Vintage Books, 1972), 46.
2 I offer this personal anecdote as the launching point for my exploration of white supremacy in the American church in *Witnessing Whiteness: Confronting White Supremacy in the American Church* (New York: Oxford University Press, 2020). Portions of this chapter appeared in my article, "James Cone's Legacy for White Christians," *Political Theology* 21, no. 3 (2020), reused here with permission.
3 Robert P. Jones, *White Too Long: The Legacy of white Supremacy in American Christianity* (New York: Simon & Schuster, 2020), 6, 169.
4 Michael Emerson and Glen Bracey, *The Religion of Whiteness: How Racism Distorts Christian Faith* (Oxford, UK: Oxford University Press, 2024).
5 Eduardo Bonilla-Silva, *Racism Without Racists: Color-Blind Racism and the Persistence of Racial Inequality in America* (Lanham, MD: Rowman & Littlefield Publishers, 2006), 2.
6 Kelly Brown Douglas, *Stand Your Ground* (New York: Orbis Books, 2017), 227.
7 Bonilla-Silva, 27–34. For a study of the ways the criminal justice system creates tropes of Black criminality that further justify prejudiced policies and treatment, see Muhammad Khalil Gibran, *Condemnation of Blackness: Race, Crime, and the Making of Modern Urban America* (Cambridge, MA: Harvard University Press, 2017).
8 Robin DiAngelo, "White Fragility," *International Journal of Critical Pedagogy* 3, no. 3 (2011): 61.
9 Thor Berger presents substantial evidence that areas with more prevalent slavery at the outbreak of the Civil War exhibit substantially less upward mobility today (Berger, "Places of Persistence: Slavery and the Geography of Intergenerational Mobility in the United States," *Demography* 55, no. 4 (2018): 1547–65).
10 Bonilla-Silva, 64–74.
11 Bonilla-Silva, 60.
12 Charles Mills, *The Racial Contract* (Ithaca, NY: Cornell University Press, 1997), 59.
13 DiAngelo, "White Fragility," 56.
14 Ruth Frankenburg, *The Social Construction of Whiteness: White Women, Race Matters* (Minneapolis: University of Minnesota Press, 1993), 1 (italics added for emphasis).

15 Bonilla-Silva, 129.
16 James Cone, *The Cross and the Lynching Tree* (Maryknoll, NY: Orbis Books, 2011), 159.
17 Joe R. Feagin and Eileen O'Brien, *White Men on Race: Power, Privilege, and the Shaping of Cultural Consciousness* (Boston: Beacon Press, 2004), 5.
18 Richard Dyer, *White: Essays on Race and Culture* (New York: Routledge, 1997).
19 James Cone, *God of the Oppressed* (Maryknoll, NY: Orbis Books, 1973), 126.
20 James W. Perkinson, *White Theology: Outing Supremacy in Modernity* (New York: Palgrave Macmillan, 2004), 153.
21 Emilie Townes, *Womanist Ethics and the Cultural Production of Evil* (New York: Palgrave Macmillan, 2006), 72.
22 Townes, 70.
23 James Baldwin, *The Fire Next Time* (New York: Vintage Books, 1962), 165.
24 Townes, 113.
25 "We are often trapped in our unexamined particularities," Townes says. "My point is that this makes us dangerous when from this stance we then try to shape public policies that affect the nation and the world" (113).
26 Robin DiAngelo similarly observes, "Universalism assumes that whites and people of color have the same realities, the same experiences in the same contexts, . . . the same responses from others, and assumes that the same doors are open to all" ("White Fragility," 59).
27 Jennifer Harvey, *Dear White Christians: For Those Still Longing for Racial Reconciliation* (Grand Rapids, MI: Eerdmans Publishing, 2014), 77.
28 James Cone, *Black Theology and Black Power* (Maryknoll, NY: Orbis Books, 1969), 144.
29 Cone, *Black Theology and Black Power*, 145.
30 The concept of reconciliation may one day prove retrievable, but as Willie Jennings writes, "before we theologians can interpret the depths of the divine action of reconciliation we must first articulate the profound deformities of Christian intimacy and identity in modernity" (Willie Jennings, *The Christian Imagination* (New Haven, CT: Yale University Press, 2010), 10).

31 Gerardo Marti, "Racial Justice and Racialized Religion: Are Progressive White Christians Getting It Right?," *Sociology of Religion: A Quarterly Review* 85, no. 3 (2024): 251–73, 260. For more, see forthcoming: Marti, Gerardo, Mark Mulder, Kevin Dougherty, Racial Justice in White Progressive Churches: Antiracism and the Limits of Inclusivity (Oxford: Oxford University Press, 2026).

32 Marti, 261.

33 Cone, *Black Theology and Black Power*, 150.

34 See Robin DiAngelo, *White Fragility: Why It's So Hard for White People to Talk about Racism* (Boston: Beacon Press, 2018).

35 James H. Cone, "The Cry of Black Blood," Martin Luther King Lecture at Duke Divinity School, April 1, 2015.

36 Cone, *God of the Oppressed*, 222. In *God of the Oppressed*, he allows that this conversion event is indeed rare (221).

37 Cone, *God of the Oppressed*, 242–3.

38 Cone, *God of the Oppressed*, 221; quoting Alan Richardson, *A Theological Word Book of the Bible* (New York: Macmillan Publishing, 1960), 191.

39 As white theologian Jennifer Harvey puts it, it is only reparations that "makes possible a repentance- and repair-based, structural response to the conditions that shape and form our racial lives in relationship with one another, with a serious and unflinching engagement of the shared histories and contemporary condition out of which those relationships emerge" (*Dear White Christians*, 171–2).

40 Robert P. Jones, *The End of White Christian America* (New York: Simon & Schuster, 2016) and "The Rage of White Christian America," *New York Times*, November 10, 2016.

41 Jonathan Tran, "Moral Innovation and Ambiguity in Asian American Christianity," *Theology Today* 75, no. 3 (2018): 347–57.

42 Kelly Brown Douglas, *What's Faith Got To Do With It? Black Bodies/Christian Souls* (Maryknoll, NY: Orbis Books, 2005), xiii.

43 James H. Cone, "Theology's Great Sin: Silence in the Face of White Supremacy," *Black Theology* 2, no. 2 (2004): 139–52.

44 Marti and Brian Harrington, "Progressive White Churches Resist Racism Too," *Faith and Leadership* (October 1, 2024): https://faithandleadership.com/progressive-white-churches-resist-anti-racism-too.

9

Climate Change

Introduction: The End of the World

I grew up Evangelical fundamentalist, so we talked about the end of the world a lot. The forces of evil would only grow stronger, and the repression of Christians would only get worse until at some point the government would take away our Bibles and declare Christianity illegal. There was almost a fetishization of apocalyptic martyrdom: we would all face the same choice as the early Christians under the Roman Empire—reject our faith or risk death. Or, if we somehow survived this tribulation, we would be taken up in rapturous glory—our bodies would disappear while our souls rose to heaven—and then the sinners who were left behind would be saved by Kirk Cameron, or something like that. In some narratives, the rapture occurred before the Great Tribulation, sometimes after; and in some accounts, our bodies actually rose into the skies as a visible witness to our righteousness, and in others, they vanished amid a mass of empty vehicles and laundry. We were not always clear on what would happen, but we were very passionate about it!

Today, I'm a bit more agnostic about what the end of the world will look like. With the possibility that in the future, humanity will be scattered across several colonized planets or that artificial intelligence will trap our brains in a simulation *Matrix*-style, and with the remains of most of deceased humanity now broken up, composted, existing as fertilizer for a tree, or as particles in our food, or ingested into our own bodies, I want to believe in the resurrection of the body, but the logistical science of that seems dubious. I no longer believe in a rapture or a version of human history that continues to worsen into some dispensationalist, dystopic reality. In fact, though on most days it may not feel like it, by all accounts—in terms of health, scientific development, and human rights—we are living in the best time to be alive in the history of the planet.

Yet, it also feels like we are in a race between human prosperity and progress *and* the progressive destruction of the planet by climate change. Most climate scientists believe we have already passed a climate change threshold—there is no going back and no reversing some of the impacts that have already been set into motion.

The 2018 report of the Intergovernmental Panel on Climate Change, the UN's body of climate scientists, declares it basically inevitable that global temperature will rise 1.5 degrees Celsius over its pre-industrial level sometime in the next twenty years, leading to more cyclones, droughts, and sea level rise, a decline in coral reefs of up to 90 percent, and considerable health risks to vulnerable populations. And this will occur regardless of *any* action we take now—we have already triggered this inevitable outcome. The scientists who issued this report are just hoping to prevent a rise of 2 degrees, that is, to *limit* the rise to just 1.5 degrees. But in their 2024 update, UN scientists warned that the world is on pace for a 2.6 degree increase by the end of the century (4.7 degrees Fahrenheit) and that only a "quantum leap in ambition" would limit it to under 2.[1] A rise to 2 degrees would damage the ecosystem of 50 percent more territory than just 1.5, and it would destroy nearly 100 percent of the coral reefs and double the risks to plant life, marine life, and vertebrae life. But just to limit temperature rise to 1.5 instead of 2 degrees will require the world to reduce CO_2 emissions by 45 percent by the year 2030—just four years from now.

The situation feels dire, and just as with the issue of racial justice, I would argue that Christianity is largely to blame for our current situation. Along with industrial capitalism, it may be the largest culprit of environmental degradation since the Industrial Revolution, and as the problem gets more urgent, our distance from any real solution only increases. Rabbi Daniel Swartz, in a history of Jewish relations to the Earth, begins:

> Once upon a time—but this is neither a fairly tale nor a bedtime story—we knew less about the natural world than we do today. Much less. But we understood that world better, much better,

for we lived ever so much closer to its rhythms. Most of us have wandered far from that earlier understanding, from our long-ago intimacy. We take for granted what our ancestors could not, dared not, take for granted; we have set ourselves apart from the world of the seasons, the world of floods and rainbows and new moons. Acknowledging our loss, we can't simply reverse course, pretend to innocence in order to rediscover intimacy. Too much has intervened.[2]

This raises the question of what Christians can and ought to do about it.

Christian Approaches to Ecology

The Bible, the origin of our faith and practice, begins in a Garden with God as the original and eternal Gardener; God, walking through the garden in the cool of the evening. As Psalm 65 sings to God, "You visit the earth and water it, you greatly enrich it; you provide the people with grain; you water its furrows abundantly, and bless its growth." And in response, the pastures, hills, meadows, and valleys shout and sing together for joy. The Creation story in Genesis 2 attends to the dirt, to soil, as its central character—the very substance from which humans are shaped and given life. As beings made in the image of God, we are bound to the Earth beneath us, to the soil and all that sprouts from it. From the beginning, humankind was one part of creation eternally connected to the rest. While many have taken the English translation of *dominion* and *subduing* as a literal mandate, the greater theme from the Genesis accounts is humanity as caretaker. As Norman Wirzba says, "Our identity and vocation as human beings made in the image of God the Gardener is for us to garden the world. We are charged to take care of soil, water, plants, and animals not as punishment but as an invitation to participate in God's own life-furthering ways with the world."[3]

Rabbi Swartz reminds us that both Judaism and Christianity have the conceptual resources to draw us close to the natural world once again. He says, "The Bible is the story of people who cared about and knew intimately the world around them."[4] The Bible is full of natural and agricultural metaphors, from the fragrant vines and the fawns of the Song of Songs, to the lion and lamb napping together in Isaiah, to the laborers working the vineyards and the rocks crying out praise to God in the Gospels. The Bible is not only the story of God or of us; it is the story of the Earth and the relationship of God and us to the Earth. And as God says in Genesis 1, all of it *is good*.

The problem is that most of Christian theology and ethics, at least until recently, has ignored this fact—we've forgotten that care for the Earth is a central ingredient of our faith and tradition. Recall Paul's words to the Romans, "Do not be conformed to this world" (Rom. 12:2). While susceptible to many interpretations, such proclamations have easily and obviously led to the belief in human separateness from the rest of creation. The Earth is ultimately not our home—we have been told. We are citizens of the city of God, the kingdom of heaven; we are strangers and pilgrims progressing through this earthly life on our way to our new heavenly home. And it is impossible to overestimate the historical impact of this Christian belief. And now we find ourselves in the middle of a crisis.

The influential philosopher, John Passmore, who began signaling alarms about the climate crisis in the 1970s, wrote that Christianity is incapable of reshaping itself in an ecologically helpful way without ceasing to be Christian.[5] Though delivering an unrelenting critique of Christianity in his groundbreaking 1967 essay, *The Historical Roots of Our Ecological Crisis*, historian Lynn White still maintains this possibility. He criticizes Christianity as "the most anthropocentric religion the world has ever seen," but argues that, "since the roots of our trouble are so largely religious, the remedy must also be essentially religious."[6] And therefore, "More science and more technology are not going to get us out of the present ecological crisis until we find a new religion, *or* rethink our old one."[7]

And while all of Christianity possesses some blame for environmental harm, I think it is safe to say that Protestantism has perpetuated the most harm to the environment, or at least proposes the most theological challenges to environmental justice. Protestant theologian John Cobb says that "Following Kant, Protestant theologians abandoned the world of nature to the sciences and took history as their only domain, usually emphasizing the moral and spiritual spheres and focusing attention on the individual person." He argues that in Protestantism's acute focus on the individual, "The doctrine of creation that had previously connected Christian thought to the whole of nature was reinterpreted to express the individual's radical dependence on God."[8] With such a sharp and unrelenting focus on eternal salvation, attention to nature became theologically irrelevant. In light of this reality, the question then becomes not one of Christian responsibility for the problem, but of our ability to address it effectively.

Drawing on and expanding upon Roman Catholic theologian John Haught, I identify four conventional approaches that Christians have taken toward ecology and environmentalism.[9]

1. The first is *apologetic*: searching the Christian tradition for ecological resources already present within, even if underused. This model argues that there is a sufficient basis in Christian sources for a response without requiring a radical transformation of the tradition. It prioritizes the notion of *stewardship*, as a better understanding of the human relation to creation than "dominion."

2. A closely related model is *anthropocentric*: caring for creation and engaging ecological issues because of the harm environmental damage causes for humans. This is not just a conservative, Evangelical method, though it is the model most Evangelical creation care activists advocate. It is also the model for many liberation theologians as well—linking environmental and social justice—and even for some ecofeminists, a perspective we will examine shortly.

3. The third model is *sacramental*: understanding the sacredness of creation and nature as a sacrament that reveals aspects of God's character to us. Advocates of this approach see the other models as too anthropocentric and attempt to refocus attention on Earth as sacred, or even as the Body of Christ itself. The Earth is central and humanity moves to the periphery of our concern; humans are derivative of the Earth. We have a moral imperative to care for the Earth for its own sake, not just because of the harm environmental damage causes to humans.

4. A newer approach, and the one advocated by Haught, is the *eschatological* approach: re-inscribing the Earth as our ultimate promise rather than an object for our ultimate escape. I'll also come back to this one at the end of this chapter.

The ethical question lurking behind all of these approaches is the relationship of, and often the tension between, care for creation and care for humanity. And this is the key tension that a communitarian virtue ethic of liberation highlights. As privileged Christians become shaped and formed by a liberative ethic, this tension between environmental and social justice arises. This is expressed in the title of a Leonardo Boff essay, "Liberation Theology and Ecology: Rivals or Partners?" He observes that "Both seek liberation, a liberation of the poor . . . and a liberation of the Earth," but acknowledges that liberation theology did not emerge out of ecological concern.[10] While we recognize that environmental injustice most often ends up harming the most vulnerable populations, sometimes the preservation of nature may require sacrifices on the part of those same populations. Are environmental concerns and liberationist values compatible? Do we require less developed and formerly colonized nations to preserve their ecological resources, like rainforests, for the sake of the future of the Earth, rather than use them for their own current economic development? What concerns do we prioritize in recognizing our limited capacities for activism and advocacy, and limited financial resources to dedicate to these causes? Do we prioritize environmental concerns over urgent human or civil rights matters like voter restriction, police brutality, or poverty? Sometimes these concerns may align, but often they seem to conflict—and overwhelm.

The remainder of this chapter deals with this tension: what is the end of the Earth? That is, what on Earth is Earth for? Is it to be used and subdued for the sake of liberating oppressed humans? Is it to be revered as intrinsically sacred and preserved even at the cost of human suffering? These are difficult questions, especially for privileged Christians who do not feel the effects of either form of injustice as directly, except for occasional hurricanes disrupting our beach vacations or higher meat prices at the market. Might we discover a theological model of liberation that mends this tension?

The Challenge of Ecofeminism

One of the most significant interventions into the way Christians approach environmental issues is called ecofeminism, and I believe ecofeminism and ecowomanism are best suited for holding together liberationist and environmental concerns—ecofeminism emerging from the (mostly white) feminist movement concerned with patriarchy and ecowomanism from the perspective of Black women struggling against the intersecting oppressions of patriarchy and racism. Both see the connection between threats to the environment and those to marginalized communities. These movements did not originate within Christianity, but are the result of broadly Christian feminist theologians drawing on resources outside of the tradition to make an intervention into Christian feminism and Christian theology more broadly. It is an attempt to revise parts of the tradition to be more attuned to the historic dual oppression of women and nature. It argues that there are important connections—historical, experiential, empirical, symbolic, and conceptual—between the domination of women and the domination of nature.

Ecofeminism and ecowomanism offer similar frameworks for developing an environmental ethic that seriously addresses the connections between these twin subordinations. This connection operates on two levels. First, it addresses the real, concrete, and disproportionate impact environmental harm has on women's lives. Data shows that around the world, women are the principal farm laborers and that especially poor, rural women in less developed countries who serve as heads of household suffer disproportionately from the harms caused by such environmental problems as deforestation, water pollution, and environmental toxins. This identifies such environmental issues as concrete feminist issues. For example, consider the ways deforestation in India impacts rural women's ability to provide for their households by destroying the resources that provide much of their indigenous food, medicine, and income-generating resources.[11]

But ecofeminists highlight the connections between feminism and ecology on the conceptual and framework level, as well. As ecofeminist Karen Warren notes, a conceptual framework is a set of basic beliefs, values, attitudes, and assumptions that shape and reflect how one sees oneself and one's world. Some conceptual frameworks are *oppressive*—they function to explain, maintain, and "justify" institutions, relationships, and practices of domination and subordination.[12] When an oppressive conceptual framework is *patriarchal*, it functions to justify the subordination of women by men, as examined in Chapter 7. But according to ecofeminists, this patriarchal oppressive system doesn't just subordinate women; it also dominates nature.

The oppressive patriarchal framework works this way: it identifies women with nature and the realm of the physical, and men with the realm of the mental. It then says that whatever is mental is superior to the physical (that body/mind dualism we keep encountering). Therefore, women are inferior to men because they are closer to nature, which is also inferior to men. And therefore, men must control women *and* nature and are justified in subordinating and dominating them—an ideology of domination. Within patriarchy, the feminization of nature and the naturalization of women are crucial to the historical subordination of both. And so, in response, ecofeminists very cleverly bridge the sacramental and anthropocentric models. They value nature as sacred while also seeing the ways humans, especially women, are harmed by environmental degradation. In this way, they are able to uphold humans and nature, social justice and ecojustice.

Ecofeminism maintains many of the values proposed in this book of a communitarian virtue ethic of liberation. As Warren argues, ecofeminism is a contextual ethics rooted in a communalist approach. Ecofeminism "involves a shift *from* a conception of ethics as primarily a matter of rights, rules, or principles predetermined and applied in specific cases to entities viewed as competitors in the contest of moral standing," to what she calls a conception of ethics emerging from "defining relationships." These are relationships that help constitute and define who we are as individuals and communities. For Warren, "it is not that rights, or rules, or principles are not relevant or important." But from the perspective of a contextualist ethic, "what *makes* them relevant or important is that those to whom they apply are entities *in relationship with others*."[13] It is this base of relationality—communalism—that renders ecofeminism contextual, holistic, and inclusive, as well as liberative for those struggling as a community to hold the liberation of women and of nature together.

Critique of Theology

Ecofeminist theology really began with the pioneering work of feminists like Rosemary Radford Ruether and Latin American feminist Ivone Gebara. These scholars were attuned to the connection between women's subordination and ecological degradation and were able to discern the role of masculine hierarchical Christian theology in perpetuating these twin harms. Ruether argues that ecofeminists must challenge the entire structure of the Christian story—nothing is off limits, and everything needs to be assessed for its role in domination. This leads her to reject or revise several key doctrines.

She most significantly rejects the Platonic dualism that has shaped much of Christian thought—mind and body, human and nature, spiritual and material, metaphysical and physical. All of these are linked by a dualistic logic that serves as a primary framework through which Christians have understood the world—whether it is intrinsic to the Gospel or not. Additionally, she rejects the notions of an original paradise in the Garden and a future paradise in heaven.[14] Human existence and salvation are purely immanent, contained within this world and on this Earth. When we die, we die, so we best take good care of what we have while we are living. Hoping in an eternal afterlife only generates an escapist theology. Gebara goes a step further and basically suggests that theology become exclusively ethics—"a system proposing ethical values for best relationships."[15] Christian theology is inescapably masculine and hierarchical, so we need to find other resources.

Ecowomanism

The perspective of ecowomanism provides another intervention into Christianity's history neglect of nature. It recognizes that Black people have often viewed ecological justice as a white person's issue. But just as women have been disproportionately impacted by environmental harm, so too have Black people. And just as women have had to deal with being historically negatively identified with nature, so too have Black people. Thus, the womanist philosopher bell hooks writes, "From slavery to the present day, the Black female body has been seen in Western eyes as the quintessential symbol of a 'natural' female presence that is organic, closer to nature, animalistic, primitive."¹⁶ And there are many historical examples of this. So, the issues identified by ecofeminism are only amplified and expanded in ecowomanism.

Ecowomanism enhances the fight against dualisms: it is the same underlying dualism that contributes to patriarchy, white supremacy, *and* environmental exploitation. Therefore, ecowomanism insists on an ethic of interdependence of the human and nonhuman. It also enhances the holistic nature of ecofeminism. As Karen Baker-Fletcher argues, ecowomanism draws on womanism's holistic, "both/and" approach. All parts of the ecosystem have equal, intrinsic value. We shouldn't fall prey to false dichotomies or choices. For instance, Baker-Fletcher argues that we do not have to choose between the belief that God created the universe out of nothing—*creatio ex nihilo*—or the view that God shaped creation out of primordial chaos. Though *creatio ex nihilo* is often dismissed by liberal theologians, she says that from her experience as a Black woman, and following the creed of womanist theologians like Delores Williams, we can learn from this belief that *God creates a way out of no way!* Even out of nothing.¹⁷

And with that, I think we have the most profound internal critique of Christian theology's role in environmental harm and the most serious account of the interlocking structure of domination that connects and indicts multiple aspects of our tradition. Because of this, I contend that ecofeminism, and especially with the both/and, holistic model of ecowomanism, offers the best hope for holding together and demonstrating the interconnectedness of social justice and environmental justice—connecting the sacramental and the best of the anthropocentric models. Concern for human liberation and the flourishing of creation are conjoined. And one practical example of how these concerns converge is the issue of environmental racism.

Environmental Racism

Environmental racism is a term that exposes the disproportionate placement of poisonous toxic waste facilities and landfills within impoverished communities and communities of color. A longform *Washington Post* article puts it even more directly: "Systemic racism has long influenced where major sources of pollution are located within communities." The article continues,

While White environmental groups tended to focus on wilderness and wildlife, activists fighting everything from toxic dumps in Alabama to massive oil and gas refineries in California have largely worked in the shadows. Yet, today, African Americans are exposed to 38 percent more polluted air than White Americans, and they are 75 percent more likely to live in communities that border a plant or factory.[18]

A recent example of this is the placement of Elon Musk's xAI superplant near the predominently Black Boxtown neighborhood of Memphis, TN with its thirty-five unpermitted gas turbines fueing its AI supercomputer. Residents say that they are already experiencing health problems due to the increase of air toxins released by the plant—as high as 79 percent at its peak. A local physician laments the damage already inflicted on his community in just one year and claims that this is just the latest in "a long legacy of environmental racism in Memphis—and in our country."[19]

Many proponents of activism against environmental racism place its origin in 1982 in the poor and rural Warren County, North Carolina, a place deeply personal and formative for me. This is the county in which my grandmother lived, where I spent countless summers roaming the rural farm fields and woods, unaware of the history of exploitation and activism. This is also the home of a young Ella Baker, her childhood home right on the Warren County line. It was home to her grandfather's church and farm, where, as we learned in Chapter 4, Baker developed the tools and skills for her career in grassroots political organizing. Warren County is rich with the activism of Black women.

Until 1977, PCBs or polychlorinated biphenyls had been widely used in the manufacturing of paints, plastics, and adhesives, and as industrial coolants. But after scientists discovered that, if inhaled or absorbed through the skin, the chemicals caused birth defects, cancer, and other disorders, the EPA banned them. A company in Raleigh, NC, decided to dump its stash, and for more than three months, it illegally poisoned an area of 14 surrounding counties with 30,000 gallons of PCBs. They were caught, and the state governor proposed gathering and re-dumping 10,000 truckloads of contaminated dirt in a soybean field in Warren County, a largely poor area that was nearly 60 percent Black. Emilie Townes calls these intentionally racist toxic placements "contemporary versions of lynching a whole people."[20]

"There, in a modest ranch house off Tower Road," the *Post* article continues, "lived a young, Black mother of two named Dollie Burwell. Barely 30, she was already a fierce civil rights activist, raised by sharecroppers who had instilled in her an unwavering sense of right and wrong." Her parents ensured that she memorized a formative Bible verse (Micah 6:8): "And what does the Lord require of you but to do justice, and to love kindness, and to walk humbly with your God?" Burwell said her mother "always made us believe we were the hands, the eyes, the feet of God on Earth." It wasn't enough to believe in justice; scripture said to fight for it. So Burwell assembled a small group of Black women to fight against the dump. They feared it would contaminate their groundwater and make their community a magnet for future toxic waste disposal. And one thing I know from living there is that these families' ancestors would have possessed, worked, and farmed this land since Emancipation. Like the Jewish people that Schwartz highlights, these were people who were intimately familiar with their land.

During an interview not far from the protest site, Burwell said her community was an easy target: "We were poor, we were Black and we were politically impotent." But they were not silent. The women organized gatherings at Coley Springs Baptist Church. They "did the cooking and feeding the protesters and doing the fliers and passing out fliers and calling people to make sure we had people to participate," Burwell recalled. Over the six-week protest, women lay in the path of massive dump trucks beside men. Children often protested with their parents. More than 500 people were arrested, including Burwell, who was hauled away five times. "A couple of times, I didn't even intend to get arrested," she said. "But you just saw the injustice in it all, and the next thing you know, you were blocking the trucks."

National television networks and major newspapers covered the Warren County demonstration, a first for a Black environmental protest. In poor, racially segregated communities across the country, people had been quietly fighting pollution from rail yards, coal-fired power plants, sewage treatment facilities, oil and gas refineries, and concrete batch mills. They saw their own stories playing out in the reality that Black people are nearly four times more likely to die from exposure to pollution than White people. Ben Chavis, one of the Warren County activists, reflected that though the cry of "I can't breathe" came to define the modern-day Black Lives Matter movement, "it echoes generations of environmental activists of color, including those who fought the toxic waste dump in North Carolina in 1982." Over twenty years later, the state finally cleaned up the contaminated soil.

The works of these Black women, recognizing the linkage between civil rights and ecojustice, are the embodiment of ecowomanism. Ecowomanism reveals a logic of domination, or "politics of domination" in the words of bell hooks, that maintains and interconnects all oppressive systems.[21] Ecofeminism and ecowomanism identify these interconnections and push Christianity to become a movement charged with ending all oppressions (a kind of none are free unless all are free mentality). They argue that neither the exploitation of nature nor the subordination of women can be overcome until both are overcome.

Ecowomanist Shamara Shantu Riley links this logic of domination to sociopolitical systems of fear and profit, which she claims are based on the desire of the privileged to secure themselves from vulnerability and mortality. This points to another important insight of ecofeminism and ecowomanism: rejecting the notion of original sin as disobedience—Adam and Eve disobeying God in the Garden. Rather, sin originates in the attempt to escape human mortality, finitude, and vulnerability, which leads to the desire to control and dominate—the root of hooks's account of the politics of domination. The human desire to secure ourselves against vulnerability, in Stanley Hauerwas's pithy phrasing, to "get out of life alive," causes us to overreach and dominate others out of fear for our own security. This includes the overarching logic of domination that supports exploiting women and nature. As Riley claims, distancing ourselves from nature calms our anxiety over our own mortality; control and domination give us the pretension of power over our destiny.[22] And so, overwhelming issues like climate change, before which we feel helpless, function to actually increase our desire for control in a ruthless cycle of domination from which only the both/and holistic model of ecowomanism can save us.

For these reasons I believe ecofeminism and ecowomanism are best poised to address social, racial, and gender justice concerns *as well as* environmental concerns holistically. These approaches clearly reveal the underlying ideology of domination that exploits all of these intersecting categories and hold the most promise for holistic solutions. As Townes argues, coupling civil rights with environmental rights is crucial to the sense of personal and communal wholeness celebrated in ecowomanism.[23] Yet, I see one crucial element lacking in this approach, critical to a Christian theology of liberation: the hope of future promise. Much of ecofeminism and ecowomanism is motivated by the urgency that this is all that we have—a belief that the vision of a past and future paradise only detracts from current environmental concerns. And, as I began this chapter, I agree with these thinkers on the ways an escapist, otherworldly, and individualistic view of salvation functions to distract us from care for the Earth and its most vulnerable inhabitants. But still, is there some way to hold onto this immanent urgency while also making room for an animating promise of future salvation or liberation that is so intrinsic to Christian theology? I contend that this resolution might be found by maintaining a commitment to ecowomanism while also retrieving John Haught's eschatological approach to ecology.

Ecology and Eschatology

The Catholic theologian John Haught begins his advocacy for an eschatological approach with Paul's belief that all of creation groans and yearns for redemption (Rom. 8:22). Creation and redemption are linked in a way that doesn't allow for the fundamentalist views of salvation that I began this chapter with—a belief that the end of the world is an ultimate escape from this planet to some disembodied perfection. Rather, the cosmos, *every* part of creation, is the promise, the embodiment of future fulfillment. In Revelation, God doesn't promise in the eschaton to make new things, but to make all things new (21:5). This view of eschatology serves as a recognition that the Earth is not perfect—it might be a sacramental sign of God's love— but it is incomplete. Eschatology is a promise of an Earth restored, transformed, made new; not destroyed or left behind. And so, any human destruction of, harm to, and ignorance of nature becomes a rejection of God's future promise of redemption. This is also a way of believing in the resurrection of the body, the resurrection of a human body that becomes Earth again as it dies—from dust to dust (Gen. 3:19). It is the resurrection of a body that has already become part of the fields and flowers that pollinate for the bees and feed the livestock, and so it is the resurrection of a body that produces the land of milk and honey of a future paradise.

And so here, we see that we cannot talk about the end of the world without also talking about the *end* of the world in a second sense—as in its purpose, what on Earth is the Earth for. The Earth is not a place we pass through as sojourners to a disembodied eternity. The Earth *is* sacred as a revelation of God to us, as the sacramental ecology scholars contend. But it is more. The Earth *is us*, and we are the Earth. It is part of salvation, part of redemption, part of whatever eschatological reality we will live into. The end of the world and the end of the world converge. The end of the world is the *imago dei*, the revelation of God in the redemption, salvation, and flourishing of all of creation.

This is why we can talk about the Earth as sacred. Human beings, created in the image of God the Gardener, were also created out of the very earth upon which we walk and to which our bodies, seeking resurrection, will return. God not only created this Earth, this soil, but God took on a body that was also made up of dirt and dwelt upon and as a part of Earth itself. And so, to paraphrase St. Gregory: that which God assumed in the Incarnation—the human body *and* the Earth with which it is intimately formed—God also redeems.

Conclusion: The Sacredness of the Mundane

In the beginning, God created the heavens and the Earth. The Gospel of John begins with its own creation story: "In the beginning was the Word, and the Word was with God, and the Word was God. All things came into being through the Word. And the Word became flesh and lived among us, and we have seen the glory of the Word" (Jn 1:1-4).

You could read this story as less earthy than its *Genesis* counterpart, more ethereal and spiritual. And in a way that portends many of the challenges facing Christian environmental ethics, it is. But you could also read the beautiful image of the Word taking up space among us, God embodied, made up of the Earth just like all of humankind, as a kind of sacramentalization of the very Earth Jesus takes up into himself. The Earth that the Word assumed in the Incarnation is the same Earth that will be redeemed in the eschaton. And as followers of Jesus, as those made up of the soil, of the Earth, just as he was, it is our job to guard it, to protect it like those women of Warren County fighting for their land and their lives, to love it and care for it, as the Incarnation of a promise yet to be fulfilled.

Ecofeminist Sally McFague, in talking about a sacramental vision of ecology, uses the phrase, the "sacredness of the mundane."[24] In many ways, an underlying theme of this book has been the ethics of the ordinary. The mundane, earthly, gritty ethics of the ordinary. Christianity is a faith of the ordinary; clearly, our central practice is one of eating the ordinary, earthy foods of bread and wine. So, in the face of overwhelming problems like climate change, we might begin with mundane ethical practices. Individual practices like recycling or composting can do some good, but joining together in larger ecological movements (organizing across religious differences) can do even more; advocating to our political officials for better regulations on carbon producers; working for better and cheaper alternative energy sources; refusing products that test on animals; and working for more animal rights. Eco-theologian Norman Wirzba contends that the most important ethical practice to confront climate change is simply eating responsibly, which includes eating locally sourced food, less meat and processed foods, as well as advocating for fresh produce and grocery stores in food desert neighborhoods so that others can eat healthily and more responsibly.[25] It is through these ordinary, mundane, collective actions that we become witnesses to God the Gardener and Redeemer of all Creation.

"If you can appreciate the Earth, you can appreciate the beauty of yourself. The same creator created both," writes ecowomanist poet and author Rachel Bagby. "And if I learned to take care of it, I'll also take care of myself and help take care of others."[26] Care for other humans, for their liberation, their survival, their flourishing, cannot be severed from care for the Earth from which we are all made. This must begin with a sober and unflinching recognition of all the ecological destruction that *Christianity* has wrought, and all the obstacles and challenges our *own* faith tradition poses to the preservation of the Earth. But we must also say with the womanist ethicists: God will make a way out of no way, even when that "no way" is Christianity itself.

Notes

1. UN Environment Programme, "Emissions Gap Report 2024": https://www.unep.org/resources/emissions-gap-report-2024.
2. Daniel Swartz, *To Till and To Tend: A Guide to Jewish Environmental Study and Action* (New York: The Coalition on the Environment and Jewish Life, 1995) and "Jews, Jewish Texts, and Nature: A Brief History," in *This Sacred Earth: Religion, Nature, Environ*ment, ed. Roger S. Gottlieb (London: Routledge, 2004), 92.
3. Norman Wirzba, "The Grace of Good Food and the Call to Good Farming," *Review and Expositor* 108 (Winter 2011): 61–71, 65. See also, Norman Wirzba, *The Paradise of God: Renewing Religion in an Ecological Age* (Oxford, UK: Oxford University Press, 2003).
4. Swartz, 92.
5. John Passmore, *Man's Responsibility for Nature* (New York: Scribner, 1974), 184.
6. Lynn White, "The Historical Roots of Our Ecological Crisis," *Science: New Series* 155, no. 3767 (March 10, 1967): 1203–7, 1205, 1207.
7. White, 1206.
8. John Cobb, Jr., "Protestant Theology and Deep Ecology," in *Deep Ecology and World Religions: New Essays on Sacred Ground*, ed. David Landis Barnhill and Roger S. Gottlieb (Albany: State University of New York Press, 2001), 213–28, 214.
9. Much of this is drawn from John Haught, *The Promise of Nature* (New York: Paulist Press, 1993).
10. Leonardo Boff, *Cry of the Earth, Cry of the Poor* (Maryknoll, NY: Orbis Books, 2002), 104, 105.
11. Aparimita and Deepak Mishra, "Deforestation and Women's Work Burden in the Eastern Himalayas, India: Insights from a Field Survey," *Gender, Technology and Development* 16 (2012): 299–328.
12. Karen Warren, "The Power and Promise of Ecological Feminism," *Environmental Ethics* 12 (1990): 1.
13. Warren, 10.
14. Rosemary Radford Ruether, "Ecofeminism: The Challenge to Theology," in *Christianity and Ecology: Seeking the Well-Being of Earth and Humans*, ed. Dieter T. Hessel and Rosemary Radford Ruether (Cambridge, MA: Harvard University Press, 2000), 103–6.
15. Ivone Gebara, "Ecofeminism: A Latin American Perspective," *Crosscurrents* 53 (Spring 2003): 93–103, 97.

16 bell hooks and Cornel West, *Breaking Bread: Insurgent Black Intellectual Life* (Boston: South End Press, 1991), 153.
17 Karen Baker-Fletcher, "Something or Nothing: An Eco-Womanist Essay on God, Creation, and Indispensability," in *This Sacred Earth: Religion, Nature, Environ*ment, ed. Roger S. Gottlieb (London: Routledge, 2004), 428–37, 432.
18 Darryl Fears and Brady Dennis, "'This is Environmental Racism': How a Protest in a North Carolina Farming Town Sparked a National Movement," *Washington Post* (April 6, 2021).
19 Andrew R. Chow, "Inside the Memphis Community Battling Elon Musk's xAI," *TIME Magazine* (August 13, 2025): https://time.com/7308925/elon-musk-memphis-ai-data-center/#.
20 Emilie Townes, "To Be Called Beloved: Womanist Ontology in Postmodern Refraction," in *Womanist Theological Ethics*, ed. Katie Geneva Cannon, Emilie Townes, and Angela Sims (Louisville, KY: Westminster John Knox Press, 2011), 190.
21 bell hooks, *Talking Back: Thinking Feminist, Thinking Black* (Boston: South End Press, 1989), 175.
22 Shamara Shantu Riley, "Ecology is a Sistah's Issue Too: The Politics of Emergent Afrocentric Womanism," in *This Sacred Earth*, ed. Roger S. Gottlieb (New York: Routledge, 2000), 412–25, 416.
23 Townes, 195.
24 See Sallie McFague, *The Body of God: An Ecological Theology* (Minneapolis, MN: Fortress Press, 1993).
25 See Norman Wirzba, *Food and Faith: A Theology of Eating* (Cambridge, UK: Cambridge University Press, 2011).
26 Rachel Bagby, "Daughters of Growing Things," in *Reweaving the World: The Emergence of Ecofeminism*, ed. Irene Diamond and Gloria Orenstein (San Francisco: Sierra Club Books, 1990), 242.

Epilogue

Ordinary Ethics

A few years ago, I had the pleasure of meeting Raphael Warnock, now US Senator from Georgia, shadowing and interviewing him for a previous book project. He was serving as Senior Pastor at Ebenezer Baptist Church in Atlanta, home church of Martin Luther King Sr. and Jr. after finishing his PhD under James Cone in 2006. In light of the legacy of this historic church and his own pedigree in Black Liberation Theology, I asked him about the most politically and ethically significant program at Ebenezer. Expecting him to offer some political meeting or systemic effort (in addition to the King legacy, the church had, after all, implemented a successful advocacy campaign to deliver better public transportation to the neighborhood, opened a community center for nonprofit services, and held important voter registration programs throughout its history), I was surprised when he mentioned Ebenezer's children's ministry.

In fact, he closes his book *The Divided Mind of the Black Church* by addressing the way this children's ministry is a practice in Christian ethics. There aren't many opportunities for neighborhood children to escape the poverty they see around them, he says, which has led to a high dropout rate, which leads to deeper oppression or even prison for many of them. So the church's ministry, which includes a literacy program, gives these children a voice in a world set against them from the beginning. Ministry and ethics intersecting.

He says of the church's children's ministry, "It has the potential to shake up the order of things." In his book he writes, "The efforts to educate black children by church women such as Arenia Mallory, no less than the civil disobedience of Martin Luther King, Jr., constitute a revolutionary act, bearing witness to 'the beloved community' and the coming reign of God."[1]

In a world where Christianity continues to inflict pain upon the most vulnerable in the world in the name of gaining prominence and power, it may feel quaint to point to a children's ministry as the most potent ethical program in a progressive congregation. (The current death toll in Gaza has increased to over 67,000 as I write this, many of them children killed with American-supplied weapons and with the support of American Christians; immigrant, queer, and trans communities' rights are being taken away daily, and many live in visceral fear for their safety; the climate stats cited in Chapter 9 present a bleak outlook for the lives of the coming generations.) In a world where the moral ambiguity of even the simplest gestures can be deflating, we are tempted toward big actions. (I'm sure, like poor Douglas Ewing, I have recently bought a gift for someone that involved unjust labor, environmental harm, and contributed to wealth inequality.) But Warnock reminds us that the quotidian can be revolutionary, and the mundane can be sacred, especially when the stakes seem so large and moral certainty so dim.[2]

I was reminded recently by an article from Isaac Villegas that in the Gospel accounts, after the cosmic altering events of Jesus' death and resurrection, the disciples go fishing and Jesus cooks them breakfast.[3] Following the defeat of death and birth of new creation (2 Cor. 5:17), this rag-tag band of revolutionaries return to their mundane activities of work and table fellowship. The Roman Empire still has its foot on the neck of Israel, religious authorities still impose rigid legalism upon the people, and Jesus just wants to spend time with his friends. What a strange, ordinary liberation. But perhaps this serves as a reminder that liberation is always *becoming*. It is birthed in ordinary acts of worship, in a children's ministry, in sharing a meal with friends, in listening to neighbors share their stories, in learning and allowing yourself to be changed by others—like that ordinary, liberatory story of Jesus listening to and learning from the persistent Canaanite woman, the outcast and oppressed of his society. Moral agency is an everyday reality, and for privileged Christians, there is no one-size-fits-all strategy. The work of practicing virtue for the sake of our neighbors is an everyday, ordinary activity. We can work to use our privilege or to undermine and tear down our privilege; we can join non-faith or inter-faith efforts or we can work to make our own congregations and denominations more just and socially active. Or, following the lead of womanism and ecowomanism, we can do both-and.

This book has attempted to provide a clear and compelling vision of the ethical life. Drawing on the wisdom of thinkers, ministers, and activists like Katie Cannon, James Cone, bell hooks, Stanley Hauerwas, Dietrich Bonhoeffer, Ignacio Ellacuría, Ella Baker, and Dollie Burwell, it has traced the contours of a communitarian virtue ethic of liberation. It has provided an argument for this framework as best suited to help privileged Christians work for the liberation of the oppressed and set ourselves free from the shackles of privilege along the way. It has demonstrated how someone who finds this framework compelling might begin to think and deliberate about important moral concerns today. But most importantly, I hope it has presented a case that ethics permeates all that we do. When you understand ethics to be the ways a community is formed by its practices and habits to embody its deepest commitments to justice and liberation, then almost every everyday activity becomes ethically charged. This is not a cause for stress or constant self-doubt, but a recognition that for Christians, ethics is integral to all we do and who we are. Discipleship is ethics, after all.

So, when you preach on the Trinity, sit with a family that grieves, attend a community organizing meeting, pray with that parishioner feeling politically isolated from her family, welcome the newcomer on a Sunday morning, give a children's sermon on the Good Samaritan, march in a Black Lives Matter or women's rights protest, critically question the mission of your congregation, provide a listening ear for the young person struggling with mental health, conduct a church business meeting, speak up at the town council meeting, remember that ethics is not some academic endeavor separate from theology, ministry, or worship. It is in all of these things. Challenging systems and empires or teaching little children: In the end, Christian ethics is the work of faith seeking to understand what it means to be disciples, what it looks like to live as the beloved community of God in the world.

* * *

Writing this book has been an adventure in the ordinary. Most of these chapters began as lectures for an ethics course at Virginia Theological Seminary that I co-taught with Dean Ian Markham. I want to thank Ian and all of the wonderful students in that class for their engagement and feedback on these thoughts. That feels like a lifetime ago, as since then, I have left formal academia after several anxious years of unsuccessfully navigating the tenure-track job market, relocated, shifted into nonprofit work, and become a parent. I call this project an adventure in the ordinary because it has been written and revised in the margins of ordinary life: between cooking dinner and writing grant proposals, community meetings and church committees, bike rides, toy trains, and coaching youth basketball. As a scholar and writer, I dreamed of making an extraordinary difference with my scholarship—changing hearts, minds, and moral actions through my books and teaching. Now I dream of helping my son and niece and nephew simply become people of character and justice, and hoping the same for myself. The scope of my dreams has contracted, but just as Warnock said, even training children can be ordinary, revolutionary, liberatory action.

I want to thank my editor Richard Brown for initiating this project, convincing me to do it, and, along with Victoria Shi, guiding me through a wonderful process with Bloomsbury. My co-workers at The Shalom Project, especially Rosa and Mercedes, picked up my slack while I occasionally took time off for writing and editing. I workshopped several of these chapters through presentations with church groups and editing sessions with friends. This book has highlighted friendship as one of those ordinary ways in which we cultivate virtue, and my friends have certainly tried to help me do so. I'm especially grateful for Brent, Amy, and John for trying to make me a better person for over twenty-five years! Thank you all. And most importantly, I want to thank my family. My parents, Keith and Elizabeth, cultivated (and at times, tolerated) my love for writing—my mom writing down stories dictated by a pre-K me on dot-matrix printer paper that I would later illustrate—as well as modeled a life of compassion for others. My nephew and niece, Wesley and Bethany, inspire my imagination daily with wonder and adventure. My life changed forever when I became a parent, and now my son Alfredo, myself, and our dog Ollie live each day with a new anticipation and wonder at this life together. Alfredo's joy and kindness are contagious, and he inspires the spirit of this book. I love this crazy, ordinary life with you all. As a family that experiences many privileges, my hope and prayer is that we always seek to be a people of character who, as Walter Brueggeman insists, are sent out beyond our privilege and dispatched for the sake of others.

Notes

1 Raphael Warnock, *The Divided Mind of the Black Church: Theology, Piety, and Public Witness* (New York: New York University Press, 2013), 189.
2 Sallie McFague, *The Body of God: An Ecological Theology* (Minneapolis, MN: Fortress Press, 1993).
3 Isaac Villegas, "Resurrection, then Breaskfast," *The Christian Century* (May 2025):https://www.christiancentury.org/voices/resurrection-then-breakfast.

BIBLIOGRAPHY

Aquinas, Thomas, *Summa Theologica* (Westminster: Christian Classics, 1981).
Augustine, *City of God*, ed. R.W. Dyson (Cambridge, UK: Cambridge University Press, 1998).
Baldwin, James. *The Fire Next Time* (New York: Vintage International, 1962).
Baldwin, James. *No Name in the Street* (New York: Vintage Books, 1972).
Barber, William J. with Jonathan Wilson-Hartgrove. *The Third Reconstruction: Moral Mondays, Fusion Politics, and the Rise of a New Justice Movement* (Boston, MA: Beacon Press, 2016).
Boff, Leonardo. *Cry of the Earth, Cry of the Poor* (Maryknoll, NY: Orbis Books, 2002).
Bonhoeffer, Dietrich. Discipleship, Dietrich Bonhoeffer Works (English), vol. 4, ed. J. Godsey and G. Kelly, trans. R. Krauss and B. Green (Minneapolis, MN: Fortress Press, 2003).
Bonhoeffer, Dietrich. Life Together and Prayerbook of the Bible, DBWE 5, ed. Geoffrey B. Kelly, trans. James H. Burtness and Daniel W. Bloesch (Minneapolis, MN: Fortress Press, 2005).
Bonilla-Silva, Eduardo. *Racism Without Racists: Color-Blind Racism and the Persistence of Racial Inequality in America* (Lanham, MD: Rowman & Littlefield Publishers, 2006).
Bretherton, Luke. *Resurrecting Democracy: Faith, Citizenship, and the Politics of a Common Life* (Cambridge, UK: Cambridge University Press, 2015).
Brown, Wendy. *States of Injury* (Princeton, NJ: Princeton University Press, 1995).
Brueggemann, Walter. *Prayers for a Privileged People* (Nashville, TN: Abingdon Press, 2008).
Butler, Judith. *Frames of War: When is Life Grievable?* (Brooklyn, NY: Verso, 2009).
Cahill, Lisa. *Blessed are the Peacemakers: Pacifism, Just War, and Peacebuilding* (Minneapolis, MN: Fortress Press, 2019).
Cannon, Katie G. *Black Womanist Ethics* (Atlanta, GA: Scholars Press, 1988).

Cannon, Katie G., Emilie Townes, and Angela Sims, eds. *Womanist Theological Ethics* (Louisville, KY: Westminster John Knox Press, 2011).
Cavanaugh, William. *Torture and Eucharist: Theology Politics, and the Body of Christ* (Hoboken, NJ: Wiley-Blackwell, 1998).
Cavanaugh, William. *Theopolitical Imagination: Christian Practices of Space and Time* (London: T&T Clark, 2003).
Cavanaugh, William. *Being Consumed: Economics and Christian Desire* (Grand Rapids, MI: Eerdmans Publishing, 2008).
Clear, James. Atomic Habits: An Easy and Proven Way to Build Good Habits and Break Bad Ones (New Hyde Park, NY: Avery Publishing, 2018).
Coles, Romand. *Beyond Gated Politics: Reflections for the Possibility of Democracy* (Minneapolis: University of Minnesota Press, 2005).
Cone, James H. *God of the Oppressed* (Maryknoll, NY: Orbis Books, 1973).
Cone, James H. *For My People* (Maryknoll, NY: Orbis Books, 1984).
Cone, James H. *A Black Theology of Liberation* (Maryknoll, NY: Orbis Books, 1986).
Cone, James H. *Black Theology and Black Power* (Maryknoll, NY: Orbis Books, 1997).
Cone, James H. *The Cross and the Lynching Tree* (Maryknoll, NY: Orbis Books, 2011).
Connell, R. W. *Masculinities* (Cambridge, UK: Polity Press, 1995).
Cooper-White, Pamela. *The Psychology of Nationalism: Why People are Drawn in and How to Talk Across the Divide* (Minneapolis, MN: Fortress Press, 2022).
Copeland, M. Shawn. *Enfleshing Freedom: Body, Race, and Being* (Minneapolis, MN: Fortress Press, 2010).
DiAngelo, Robin. *White Fragility: Why It's So Hard for White People to Talk about Racism* (Boston: Beacon Press, 2018).
Douglas, Kelly Brown. *What's Faith Got to Do with It? Black Bodies/ Christian Souls* (Maryknoll, NY: Orbis Books, 2005).
Douglas, Kelly Brown. *Stand Your Ground: Black Bodies and the Justice of God* (Maryknoll, NY: Orbis Books, 2015).
Emerson, Michael and Glen Bracey. *The Religion of Whiteness: How Racism Distorts Christian Faith* (Oxford, UK: Oxford University Press, 2024).
Frankenburg, Ruth. *The Social Construction of Whiteness: White Women, Race Matters* (Minneapolis: University of Minnesota Press, 1993).
Freier, Paulo. *Pedagogy of the Oppressed* (London: Bloomsbury, 2012).
Graaff, Guido de. *Politics in Friendship: A Theological Account* (London: T&T Clark, 2014).

Grant, Joanne. *Ella Baker: Freedom Bound* (New York: John Wiley & Sons, 1998).
Guth, Karen V. *The Ethics of Tainted Legacies: Human Flourishing After Traumatic Pasts* (Cambridge, UK: Cambridge University Press, 2022).
Gutiérrez, Gustavo. *The Power of the Poor in History* (Maryknoll, NY: Orbis Books, 1983).
Gutiérrez, Gustavo. *A Theology of Liberation: History, Politics and Salvation* (Maryknoll, NY: Orbis Books, 1988, orig. 1973).
Harris, Melanie. *Gifts of Virtue, Alice Walker, and Womanist Ethics* (Basingstoke, UK: Palgrave McMillan, 2010).
Hartman Saidiya. *Lose Your Mother: A Journey Along the Atlantic Slave Route* (New York: Farrar, Straus & Giroux, 2008).
Harvey, Jennifer. *Dear White Christians: For Those Still Longing for Racial Reconciliation* (Grand Rapids, MI: Eerdmans Publishing, 2014).
Hauerwas, Stanley. *A Community of Character: Toward a Constructive Christian Social Ethic* (Notre Dame, IN: University of Notre Dame Press, 1981).
Hauerwas, Stanley and Sam Wells, eds. *Blackwell Companion to Christian Ethics* (Oxford, UK: Blackwell, 2004).
hooks, bell. *Talking Back: Thinking Feminist, Thinking Black* (Boston: South End Press, 1989).
hooks, bell. *The Will to Change: Men, Masculinity, and Love* (New York: Washington Square Press, 2004).
Jennings, Willie. *The Christian Imagination* (New Haven, CT: Yale University Press, 2011).
Jones, Robert P. *White Too Long: The Legacy of white Supremacy in American Christianity* (New York: Simon & Schuster, 2020).
Luther, Martin. *On Christian Liberty*, trans. W. A. Lambert (Minneapolis, MN: Fortress Press, 2003).
Mansfield, Harvey C. *Manliness* (New Haven, CT: Yale University Press, 2006).
Marsh, Charles. *Strange Glory: A Life of Dietrich Bonhoeffer* (New York: Alfred Knopf, 2016).
McFague, Sallie. *The Body of God: An Ecological Theology* (Minneapolis, MN: Fortress Press, 1993).
Mez, Kristin Kobes Du. *Jesus and John Wayne: How White Evangelicals Corrupted a Faith and Fractured a Nation* (New York: Liveright Press, 2020).
Moye, J. Todd. *Ella Baker: Community Organizer of the Civil Rights Movement* (New York: Rowman & Littlefield, 2013).
O'Donovan, Oliver and Joan Lockwood O'Donovan, *From Irenaus to Grotius: A Sourcebook in Christian Political Thought* (Grand Rapids, MI: Eerdmans Publishing, 1999).

Payne, Charles. *I've Got the Light of Freedom: The Organizing Tradition and the Mississippi Freedom Struggle* (Berkeley: University of California Press, 2007).

Putnam, Robert and David Campbell, *American Grace: How Religion Divides and Unites Us* (New York: Simon & Schuster, 2012).

Ransby, Barbara. *Ella Baker and the Black Freedom Movement: A Radical Democratic Vision* (Chapel Hill: University of North Carolina Press, 2003).

Romero, Oscar. *Voice of the Voiceless: Four Pastoral Letters and Other Statements* (Maryknoll, NY: Orbis Books, 1985).

Smith, James K. A. *Desiring the Kingdom: Worship, Worldview, and Cultural Formation* (Grand Rapids, MI: Baker Academic, 2009).

Smith, James K. A. *Awaiting the King: Reforming Public Theology* (Grand Rapids, MI: Baker Publishing, 2017).

Sobrino, Jon. *No Salvation Outside the Poor: Prophetic-Utopian Essays* (Maryknoll, NY: Orbis Books, 2008).

Stassen, Glen. Just Peacemaking: Transforming Initiatives for Justice and Peace (Louisville, KY: Westminster John Knox Press, 1992).

Stout, Jeffrey. *Blessed Are the Organized: Grassroots Democracy in America* (Princeton, NY: Princeton University Press, 2010).

Stringfellow, William. *My People is the Enemy: An Autobiographical Polemic* (Eugene, OR: Wipf and Stock, 2005).

Tessman, Lisa. *Burdened Virtues: Virtue Ethics for Liberatory Struggles* (Oxford, UK: Oxford University Press, 2005).

Thurman, Howard. *Jesus and the Disinherited* (Boston: Beacon Press, 1996).

Townes, Emilie. *Womanist Ethics and the Cultural Production of Evil* (Basingstoke, UK: Palgrave MacMillan, 2007).

Volf, Miroslav, Matthew Croasmun, and Ryan McAnnally-Linz. *Life Worth Living: A Guide to What Matters Most* (New York: The Open Field, 2023).

Warnock Raphael. *The Divided Mind of the Black Church: Theology, Piety, and Public Witness* (New York: New York University Press, 2013).

Wells, Samuel. *Improvisation: The Drama of Christian Ethics* (Grand Rapids, MI: Brazos Press, 2004).

West, Traci. *Disruptive Christian Ethics: When Racism and Women's Lives Matter* (Louisville, KY: Westminster John Knox Press, 2006).

Winner, Lauren. *The Dangers of Christian Practice: On Wayward Gifts, Characteristic Damage, and Sin* (New Haven, CT: Yale University Press, 2018).

Wirzba, Norman. *The Paradise of God: Renewing Religion in an Ecological Age* (Oxford, UK: Oxford University Press, 2003).

INDEX OF BIBLICAL REFERENCES

Gen.
  1-2 169–170
  3 134
  3:19 180
  16 134

Exod.
  23:10-11 119

Lev.
  23:22 119
  25:8-22 3

Num.
  13:25-31 67

Deut.
  21 134

Psalm
  19:3 45
  65 169

Prov.
  14:31 119
  28:27 119

Isa.
  11:6-9 158

Jer.
  6:14 163
  29:7 92

Amos
  6:21 1

Micah
  6:8 178

Mt.
  5:24 65
  5:43-46 37–40
  5:48 40
  10:34 41
  12:30 22
  13:22 1, 20
  15:21-28 20–21
  18:3 81
  19:23 81
  20:25-26 81
  21:31 81

Mk
  7:24-30 20–21
  8:34 159
  8:35 139
  9:40 22
  10:14 81
  10:23 81

12 82
15:26 81
Lk.
  4:16-19 80
  4:18-21 3
  6:20 81, 119
  18:16 81
  18:24-25 81
  19 161
Jn.
  1:1-4 181
  14:27 42
Acts
  2:1-13 81
  10:34 155

Rom.
  7:19 60
  8:22 180
  12:2 170
  13 82
1 Cor.
  11:17-33 60
  13:12 18, 44

2 Cor.
  5:17 186
  5:18-19 157
Eph.
  2:14 81
  5:22 134
Phil.
  2:5-11 81
1 Tim.
  2:12 134
2 Tim.
  3:16 41

Heb.
  5:14 57
James
  2:17 58
1 Pet.
  1:3 31
Rev.
  1:5 82
  5:6-7 81
  13 82
  21:5 180

INDEX

Anabaptism 7
Aquinas, Thomas 102, 123
Arendt, Hannah 144
Aristotle 39–40, 44, 47–8, 59, 121
Atlantic Slave Trade 2–4, 62–4, 120–1
Augustine 59, 73, 82–3, 92, 98–100, 102, 104–5, 118, 120, 122

Baker, Ella 77–9, 87–92, 177, 187
Baldwin, James 143, 149–50, 156
baptism 2–3, 19, 43, 64, 66, 68
Barber, William 117, 126–8
Beatles, The 69, 122
Black liberation theology 7, 23, 26–8, 63–7, 107–9, 158–62, 185
Black Lives Matter 1, 66, 71, 179, 187
Bonhoeffer, Dietrich 9, 15–16, 25–6, 28–32, 46, 51, 58, 92, 124, 144–5, 187
Bonilla-Silva, Eduardo 152
Brueggeman, Walter 5–6, 188
Butler, Judith 110–11

Cahill, Lisa 98, 103, 106, 110–11

Calvin, John 83–5
Canaanite/Syrophoenician woman 20, 69, 71, 186
Cannon, Katie 23–6, 45, 48, 187
capitalism 1, 118–22, 168
Cavanaugh, William 101, 119
Christian nationalism 84–7, 92
Civil Rights Movement 8, 26, 58, 77–9, 87–91
colorblindness 1, 150–6, 160, 163
communitarian virtue ethic of liberation 8–9, 18, 46–51, 56, 68–72, 88, 110–11, 141, 159, 172, 174, 187
community organizing 77–9, 87–92, 126–7, 177, 187
Cone, James 7, 26–8, 41–4, 58, 80, 107–11, 122, 139, 154, 157, 159–63, 185, 187
consequentialism 38–9
context 8–9, 22–31, 69–70, 107–11, 174
Copeland, M. Shawn 65, 125, 159

deontology 36–8, 47
DiAngelo, Robin 153
Didache, the 18–19, 26, 57, 82
Douglas, Kelly Brown 4, 63, 120–1, 151, 162
Du Mez, Kristin Kobes 135

INDEX

dualism 175–6
duty, *see* deontology
ecofeminism 1, 171, 173–6, 179–80, 186
ecowomanism 1, 173–6, 179–80, 182, 186
Ellacuría, Ignacio 115–16, 118, 128, 187
environmental racism 176–80
Eucharist/Communion 19, 56, 60, 62–6, 68
Evangelicalism 17, 84–6, 131–2, 135–6, 138, 167

feminist theology 139–40, 173–6
formation, moral 28–31, 48–50, 57–68, 71, 79, 91–2, 110–11, 119–22, 187
Freire, Paulo 91
friendship 142–5, 188

Good Place, The 35–6, 38, 47
Guth, Karen 29, 52
Gutiérrez, Gustavo 26–7, 80–1, 92, 123

habits 39–40, 55–62, 71
Harvey, Jennifer 157
Hauerwas, Stanley 48, 57, 98, 144–5, 179, 187
hooks, bell 134, 139, 141–2, 175, 179

individualism 43, 70, 180
Industrial Areas Foundation (IAF) 77–9, 88

Jennings, Willie 63, 81, 165
Jubilee 3
just peacebuilding/peacemaking 106, 111
just war theory 98–106, 109–11

Kant, Immanuel 37, 44, 170
King Martin Luther Jr. 47, 66–7, 78, 89–90, 109, 185

liberation theology 7–8, 26–8, 46, 49–50, 69–72, 107–9, 115–16, 118, 122–6, 171–2, 180
loneliness 140–1, 143
Luther, Martin 40, 42, 83–5, 98, 100–1

Marti, Gerardo 158–9, 163
McFague, Sally 182
Mill, John Stuart 38, 44
Moral Mondays 117, 126–8

Niebuhr, Reinhold 38–9, 98, 101–2

pacifism 98–101, 104–8, 110–11
Peeps 36
Pentecost 81
Pope Francis 104–5
postliberalism 7–8, 17–20, 69–72
practices, Christian 29–30, 55–68, 71, 107, 143, 182, 187
prayer 5, 6, 9, 19, 30, 43, 58–9, 64, 124, 131, 149, 188
preferential option for the poor 122–5

Racism Index 150
Rambo, Shelly 101, 108
Rauschenbusch, Walter 135
Realism, Christian 7, 38–9, 101
reconciliation, racial 150, 156–8, 163, 165
reparations 30, 161–3, 166
repentance 23, 30–2, 65, 67–8, 125, 161–2

responsibility, ethics of 25, 29–31, 49–51, 110–11, 134, 139, 141–5
results, *see* consequentialism
Romero, Oscar 109, 115, 124

Sermon on the Mount 37–40, 83, 100
Smith, James K. A. 60, 62–3, 119–20
Sobrino, Jon 115, 124–6, 128
Social Gospel 7, 85, 135
solidarity 79, 115, 122–7, 139–40, 157, 159, 161–2
Stringfellow, William 6
Student Nonviolent Coordinating Committee (SNCC) 78, 90–1
suffering 23–4, 30, 50, 66, 118–22, 124–5, 160, 172

Tessman, Lisa 49–50
Thurman, Howard 4
Tocqueville, Alexis de 79
Townes, Emilie 28, 30, 79–80, 155–6, 165, 177–8, 180
toxic masculinity 132–4, 137, 143
tradition 43–4

ubuntu 47

UN Intergovernmental Panel on Climate Change 168

virtue ethics 7–9, 39–40, 46–51, 55–62, 69–72, 92, 188
"burdened virtues" 49
womanist virtue ethics 40, 48–51
Volf, Miroslav 72

Warnock, Raphael 67, 185–6, 188
Warren County, NC/Littleton, NC 78–9, 177–9, 182
Wells, Sam 57, 60–1
West, Traci 58, 64, 66
White, Lynn 170
Whiteness 30, 63, 121, 150, 159–61
definition of 153, 156, 160
uninterrogated 155–6
Williams, Delores 176
Winner, Lauren 64
Wirzba, Norman 169, 182
witness 16–18, 22–3, 41–5, 69
womanist ethics 8, 24–6, 28–30, 40, 48, 65–6, 69, 141, 145
Wright, N. T. 81

Yoda 47

ABOUT THE AUTHOR

Kristopher Norris, PhD, is the author of three books: *Witnessing Whiteness: Confronting White Supremacy in the American Church*, *Kingdom Politics*, and *Pilgrim Practices*. He has served as Visiting Distinguished Professor of Public Theology and consultant for the Center for Public Theology at Wesley Theological Seminary, as well as the Kreitler Visiting Professor of Christian Ethics at Virginia Theological Seminary. He currently works in the nonprofit sector and serves as Vice President of the Alliance of Baptists.